American Trails Series
XV

Other works by Albert Shumate —

The Life of George Henry Goddard (1969)
The California of George Gordon (1976)
Francisco Pacheco of Pacheco Pass (1976)
Mariano Malarin, a Life that Spanned Two Cultures (1980)
Boyhood Days, Ygnacio Villegas' Reminiscences (1983)

A lithograph by F. Kuhl who was in San Francisco, 1857-1858. On the left at top are the banks which did not fail, in the water are Adams & Co. and other failures. Wells Fargo, who had closed, soon reopened, and is shown walking up the steps from the water.

The Notorious

I . C . WOODS

of the Adams Express

by ALBERT SHUMATE

with Foreword by KEVIN STARR

THE ARTHUR H. CLARK COMPANY
Glendale, California   1986

Dedicated to
RUTH TEISER
who has rendered such great help
in preparing my monographs

Contents

Illustrations

Foreword

History is fair to some and unfair to others. Until the appearance of this volume, history has been notoriously unfair to Isaiah Churchill Woods, the San Francisco-based businessman and entrepreneur. Woods had the misfortune of being associated with Adams and Company when that banking and express agency collapsed in the Panic of 1855. As Dr. Albert Shumate honestly tells us, Woods' conduct during the run on his agency left much to be desired; but it was not — either as action or intent — blatantly criminal. Seeking to protect their employers in the midst of a panic, Woods and his colleagues cut corners and did not tell the full truth. They were dealing, however, with a situation not of their own making, and it is from this perspective that their conduct must be judged.

Woods' actions, however, were considered "notorious" by the San Francisco press; and this epithet, this persistent notoriety, as Dr. Shumate so poignantly chronicles, was destined to follow Woods throughout his life. Reading this biography, one cannot help but see in Isaiah Churchill Woods one of those men (Joseph Conrad's fictional character Lord Jim comes to mind) who are destined to spend their lives, however worthy or even heroic, running ahead of an early mistake, an early tragedy, which beclouds all subsequent effort.

This early but persistent error provides the central dramatic structure of Dr. Shumate's well-researched and elegantly written biography: how a reputation can fix itself to a man or a woman at an early date, and in turn cause future failures. From this perspective, the life of Isaiah Churchill Woods is indeed a record of disappointed and disappointing effort. His early business career collapsed with Adams and Company, earning him the derision of his contemporaries. His next effort — the establishment of a stagecoach and mail line to California across the Southwest — ended also in disappointment. When the War Between the States broke out, Woods performed brilliantly as a staff officer for Major General John Charles Fremont; but even then the finger of accusation was pointed, albeit unjustly, in his direction, and Woods' military career collapsed with the removal of Fremont from command. He next sought to establish a competing transportation route across Nicaragua. That enterprise failed in 1868. Returning to California that year, Woods threw himself back into business, this time in the lumber business. As promising as was his process for chemically treating wood for use in piers, roads, and foundations, however, the Pacific Wood Preserving Company, the beleagured Woods' last major venture, went the way of previous efforts, collapsing in 1875, the *annus mirabilis* of business failure, when William C. Ralston of the Bank of California also went broke and lost his life.

In the end, in his final years, Woods turned to the land, where he perhaps should have put his efforts in the first place. He became a vineyardist and winemaker in the area around Mission San Jose on the southeast shore of San Francisco Bay.

And yet — has Dr. Shumate written a tale of unmitigated failure? Is Woods' life as sad and dreary as the bare facts of his business ventures would seem to suggest? I personally believe that the answer to these queries must be a resounding No! In each of his activities — banking, transportation, military logistics, lumber, and wine — Woods demonstrated an element of vision that raised his business efforts beyond the commonplace, no matter how mixed or even disastrous were the concrete results of his ventures. In my opinion, Isaiah Churchill Woods — as he unfolds in these pages — typifies a major force in the creation of the Far West in general, and California in particular: the force of business vision and energy allied to indomitable will. Time and again, Woods saw what California needed in order properly to develop itself as a commonwealth. There had to be banking, a rail and stagecoach line across the Southwest, a more efficient route across Central America, and foundation piles capable of sustaining themselves in the soggy soil of the San Francisco peninsula. Woods dreamed bold dreams. More than twenty-five years ahead of the Southern Pacific, he realized that the Butterfield Trail had to be expanded into a major transportation route across the Southwest if Southern California were to have the opporunity to develop itself in tandem with the North. His efforts to establish efficient transportation across Nicaragua were also energized by a far-reaching vision, one destined to find fulfillment nearly a half century later in the completion of the Panama Canal.

History can be harsh. History also needs scapegoats. The failure of Adams and Company in the Panic of 1855 needed a scapegoat, and Woods, if the truth be told, more than made himself available. History also

requires a greater breadth and intensity of effort than
singular instances of success. It is easy to remember the
ventures that succeeded. It is slightly more challenging
to acknowledge that behind each of these successful
ventures (the transcontinental railroad is a major case
in point) there must needs be a whole host of
experiments that come to naught.

Perceived as a record of aspiration and intelligent
dreaming, the career of Isaiah Churchill Woods
becomes, not a record of disappointment, but a case
study in that special mix of vision and practicality that is
at the core of the American identity. New England-
born, raised in an atmosphere of thrift, religion, and
hard work, Woods embodies the American energies
that flooded West after 1846. In these pages, one feels
once again with Woods the excitement of this young
New Englander as he set sail in 1847 for the South
Pacific and from there, leaving Honolulu on 27
October 1848, for the new El Dorado of California.
Here, through the scholarship and narrative skills of
Albert Shumate, we re-experience the story of San
Francisco in the early 1850s, its Age of Iron, when
Woods and his fellow entrepreneurs — John Parrott,
Sam Brannan, Thomas Larkin, Frank Woods,
William T. Sherman — built up, simultaneously, a new
American metropolis and their own fortunes which
were inextricably inter-twined with its success. Here is
the frenzied atmosphere of the offices, street corners
and saloons of the city in the Panic of 1855, which left
one company, Wells Fargo, in virtual control of the
express business of the West. Here are long hot
exhausting days in the deserts of the Southwest, as
Woods endeavored to establish for Southern California

its own transportation system. Here are the heady days of staff work for General Fremont and the Army of the West, when the Pathfinder seemed surely destined for the inevitable command of the entire Union Army. Here are the steamy jungles of Nicaragua and the dream of linking Atlantic and Pacific in a more efficient manner. Here is the bustling activity of San Francisco in the 1870s, a time of speculation, fortune-making, and with the fall of the Bank of California in 1875, shocking collapse. Here, at last, are the sunny slopes of Mission San Jose, where vineyards ripen under the sun.

Putting down Dr. Shumate's biography, we must remember these times of exhilaration and hope, when the West seemed winnable and worth the winning, as well as the times of failure and despair. No — not despair; Isaiah Churchill Woods never found himself without hope, the *sine qua non* of pioneering virtues: hope that, whatever the failures of the past, the next effort, the next venture would bring the long-longed-for success.

Hope drove Americans across the trackless desert. Hope sent them sailing around the Horn in 1849. Hope sustained them as San Francisco burned to the ground, as banks and other ventures failed, as overland transportation systems collapsed against the onslaughts of heat, thirst, hostile Indians, and the immeasurable distances that stretched between settled America and the Pacific slope. Hope — pithy, uncomplaining, ever-renewing itself, ever eschewing self-pity — sustained Isaiah Churchill Woods from venture to venture; and it was with him to the last, one suspects, as he stood in his later years in a Mission San Jose vineyard, feeling the sun on his face and seeing all around him the splendid renewal of the vines that was the perfect emblem of the manner in which his own life had renewed itself from failure to failure, which was also from success to success.

KEVIN STARR

San Francisco
August 8, 1985

Acknowledgments

I wish to express my gratitude to the many wonderful people who have been of great assistance in writing this monograph.

I am especially indebted to Ruth Teiser for her aid in preparing this biography and for the valuable assistance received from Betty Gardiner.

I am most particularly grateful to a member of my camp at the Bohemian Club Grove, Kevin Starr, for writing the Foreword and to Robert and Arthur Clark, of the Arthur H. Clark Company, for the splendid taste and knowledge in editorial detail.

Special appreciation is extended to Anna Marie and Everett Hager for compiling the index and to Mrs. A.J. Fallon, granddaughter of Francis Woods, for information regarding the Woods family.

The staff at the California Historical Society's library have always been most helpful: Bruce Johnson, Douglas Haller, Judith Sheldon, and Gerald Wright.

I wish to thank Diana and Merlin Porter for their kindness in allowing me to quote from the Eugene Casserly letters in their collection.

I would like to thank Edwin Carpenter and Virginia Rust at the Huntington Library and Dr. James Hart and his staff at the Bancroft Library, especially Peter Hanff and Anthony Bliss.

In Vallejo, I am indebted to several for their

kindness: Rev. Franklin Dalton, Sue Lemmon, Genera Brownridge, and Ernest Wichels. At the Society of California Pioneers, I was aided by John Fuller, Roger Jobson, and Grace Baker. Valuable help has been rendered by Rickey Best of the San Diego Historical Society; Robin Gottfried of the National Archives at San Bruno, California; and by the staff at the San Francisco Maritime Museum. Also I wish to thank the Wells Fargo History Department staff, especially Dr. Robert Chandler and Basil Pearce.

Special aid has been obtained from Joseph Samora of the State Archives at Sacramento and from Gary Kurutz and his staff at the California State Library. Marguerite Ashford of the Bishop Museum in Hawaii has been most kind.

I am greatly obliged to many on the East Coast: from Maine, Amanda Bond of Springvale, Carole Thomas of Bath, Joan LaMontagne of Saco, and particularly Cynthia Murphy of Portland. In Massachusetts, I am grateful to the Rev. David Ransom of Fairhaven, Dr. Harold Worthley of Boston, Virginia Adams of New Bedford, and Louise Hussey of Nantucket.

I am greatly obliged to James Abajian, Mrs. Walter Bush, Herb Garcia, Dr. Jane Hamersley, Carter Keene, Dr. John Kemble, Wilber Leeds, Carol Hunley Leisy, Sister Catherine McShane, Kendrick Miller, Harry Poett, Joan and Ruth Quigley, Dorothy Regnery, Ray Siemans, Joseph Smith, Mrs. M.K. Swingle, and June Whitesides.

Preface

"The notorious I.C. Woods" was well-known to San Franciscans of the early 1850s. Before the fall of Adams & Co. in 1855, he was noted as an energetic and valuable business leader of the young gold-rush city. For many years after that disaster, however, the adjective "notorious" was attached to his name almost every time it was mentioned in the newspapers.

He was born in Saco, Maine, but was still young when his family moved to New Bedford, Massachusetts, the chief seat of the United States whale fishery. Following his sea captain father's untimely death, he went to work in his early teens. He did well as a clerk and then as a partner in a crockery and glassware store. At the age of 22, aspiring to better himself, he organized a shipping expedition to the South Seas and might have remained in the shipping business had it not been for the California gold rush. Quickly drawn to San Francisco, like so many ambitious and adventuresome young men, I.C. Woods showed special skill at the kind of speculation that the fast-growing city was thriving upon. However, he proved no more adept than many others at escaping its pitfalls. Thus when Adams & Co., the banking and express company with which he was associated, fell, taking with it the money of many depositors, his reputation fell as well, and he was labeled by the local press "the notorious I.C. Woods."

My interest in Woods was aroused by the many
newspaper references to him that I came upon while
seeking information for my biography of George
Gordon. I assumed from them that Woods was a
scoundrel and wondered what happened to him after
the disaster of 1855. When, however, I learned more of
his life before and after his early San Francisco years, I
became less certain of his villainy and finally reached
quite another conclusion. I came to believe that his
optimism and energy, although perhaps not always
coupled with untarnished ethics but still within legal
bounds, led him into that and other later failed
ventures, but that he was not a primary cause of their
failures. He became superintendent of the first
transcontinental mail line, which failed when a more
highly subsidized line on a more practical route was
sponsored by the government. In the Civil War he was
associated with General John Charles Fremont during
the "hundred days"; they ended disastrously because of
Fremont's own actions.

Woods' post-war operations in Nicaragua for a
company that planned to transport passengers across
the isthmus also ended in disappointment through no
known fault of his. In San Francisco again, he headed a
manufacturing company which seemed promising at
first, but failed when its product was found to be
defective.

Throughout Woods' mature life he was restless,
always ambitious, always seeking new ventures. It was
perhaps characteristic of him that even when he was in
poor health just before his life ended, he was
experimenting with grape vines that he hoped within
several years would make a superior wine. He died

before the success of this venture could be determined. However, by then he had outlived being referred to as "the notorious I.C. Woods" and instead was characterized as a man of "indomitable energy" and "the boldest and most brilliant" financier of gold-rush San Francisco.[1]

---

[1]*San Francisco Bulletin*, Feb. 17, 1880, in an article ten days after Woods' death.

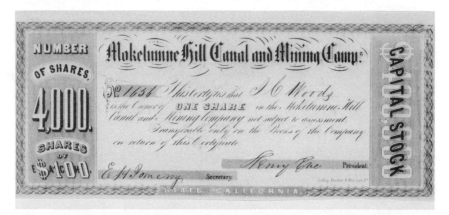

Certificate of exchange from Adams & Co. (top) and a stock
certificate for the Mokelumne Hill Canal and Mining
Company issued to I.C. Woods.
From the author's collection.

I

Flush Times

Isaiah Churchill Woods was born on October 8, 1825, in Saco, Maine.[1] He was the son and namesake of a native of Halifax, Massachusetts,[2] and the descendant of New Englanders who had fought in the American Army in the War of Independence.

His grandfather Francis Woods settled in Saco, where he served as a deacon of the Congregational Church and as a member of the Saco Health Committee.[3] Later he became superintendent of the Seaman's Mission at Portland, Maine, where he died in 1847 at the age of 67. I.C. Woods, Senior, his son, was educated at Thornton Academy of Saco and in 1824 married another New Englander, Nancy Smith of Biddleford, Maine.[4] He was a sea captain and met an untimely death at the age of 38 at St. Croix while commanding the brig *Abigail Richmond*.[5] The family was then living in New Bedford, Massachusetts.

[1] I.C. Woods' birth date is from his obituary in the San Francisco newspapers. Letters from the town clerks of Saco and Bath, Maine, from the Maine Historical Society, and from a certified genealogist, Amanda L. Bond of Springvale, Maine, failed to verify the date. Also, records of his baptism on May 19, 1839, at New Bedford's North Congregational Church (now known as the Pilgrim United Church of Christ) and of N. Gray and Co. of San Francisco, who were in charge of the funeral, fail to give the birth date of Woods.

[2] I.C. Woods, Senior, was born in Halifax, MA, Dec. 6, 1801.

[3] Francis Woods, a native of Halifax born about 1780, married Jane Churchill of Plympton, MA, on Oct. 4, 1797.

[4] Saco Records: "...declared his intention to marry" on Sept. 9, 1824.

Isaiah C. Woods, Jr., was 14 at the time of his father's death, January 30, 1839. He went to work to support his family, which consisted of his mother and his younger brothers, David and George. He was apparently a diligent young man. The *New Bedford Directory of 1841* lists him as a clerk in the crockery and glassware store of George Tappan.[6] By 1845, according to the *New Bedford Directory* of that year, he had become a partner with John H.P. Allen in another store dealing in the same kind of goods as Tappan's.[7] On November 27 of that same year he married Anna Eliza Fitch, aged 19, in the North Congregational Church of New Bedford.[8] She was the daughter of George Fitch of Nantucket, a dealer in barrels, possibly a cooper.

New Bedford was a center of shipping, and at the time was the chief seat of the United States whale fishery. Nearby Boston had been the center of the lucrative Boston-California commerce in hides and tallow. However, this trade was becoming much less profitable by 1847 because of the unsettled conditions in California caused by the war with Mexico.[9] During the gold-rush year of 1849, while most vessels left the ports of New York and Boston for California, New Bedford's importance in shipping is shown by its ranking third in number of clearances.[10]

[5]American Antiquarian Soc., *Index to Obituaries*, vol. V, 1774-1800. This St. Croix is most likely the river or town located between Maine and New Brunswick, not the Virgin Island.

[6]Hiram Woods, a brother of I.C. Woods, Senior, in 1824 married Eliza Chase, whose mother's maiden name was Elizabeth Tappan.

[7]*New Bedford Directory of 1845.*

[8]*Vital Records of New Bedford, Mass. To the Year of 1850*, Vol. II, Marriage (Boston, MA, 1932).

[9]Adele Ogden, "Boston Hide Droghers along California Shores," *Calif. Hist. Soc. Quar.*, vol. 8, no. 4 (Dec. 1929), p. 289.

[10]*Hunt's Magazine*, Feb. 1850.

We do not know why in 1847 the young Woods decided to seek his fortune in the far-away Pacific. We do know that by then he had prospered sufficiently to buy a ship and initiate a trading venture. On October 29, 1847, he voyaged from New Bedford as owner and supercargo of the schooner *Sagadahock*.[11] He sailed "'round the Horn" into the south Pacific and on October 13, 1848, arrived in Honolulu from Tahiti.[12]

In Honolulu he heard of the sensational discovery of gold in California, so on October 27, 1848, it was "Ho! For California." He set sail for the new El Dorado. On November 22 he arrived in San Francisco with much of his cargo still unsold. There he disposed of his goods at a huge profit and then proceeded to rent his ship for $2,000 a month.[13] He rented it to Colonel Jonathan D. Stevenson, who used it for surveying Suisun Bay. Stevenson was attempting to develop his new "City of New York of the Pacific" at the site of the present Pittsburg, California. Later Woods sold an interest in the *Sagadahock* to James Blair, agent for Aspinwall's Pacific Mail and son of the famous Francis Blair, of which more later.

I.C. Woods quickly established himself in San Francisco, and in early 1849 he became a member of the commercial firm of Woods and Mason. However, he soon made a trip to the States, apparently returning with the man who initiated his association with the firm of Adams & Co. It is said that on the journey he met Daniel Hale Haskell, who was traveling to California to open a branch of the well-known New

[11]*New Bedford Mercury*, Nov. 5, 1847, kindness of the Old Dartmouth Hist. Soc., Whaling Museum, New Bedford, MA.

[12]*The Friend*, Honolulu, Nov. 1, 1848, kindness of the Bishop Museum, Honolulu.

[13]*New Bedford Mercury*, Feb. 16, 1849.

This painting by John Pendergast shows Montgomery Street near California in 1851. Adams Express is located in Woods' building, three stories high with flag on top at right.

Courtesy: National Maritime Museum, San Francisco.

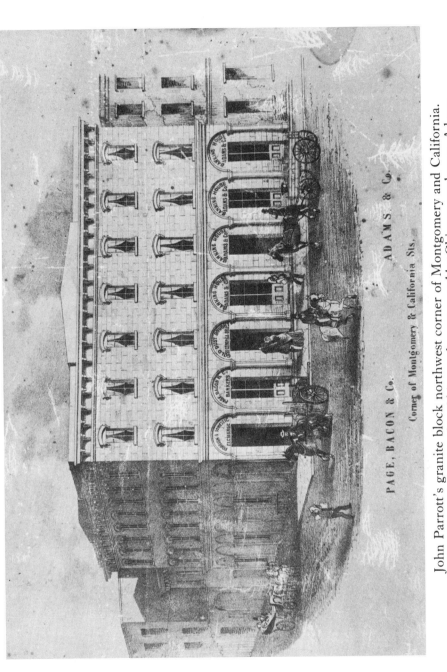

John Parrott's granite block northwest corner of Montgomery and California.
Built with stone prepared in China and constructed by Chinese workmen, Adams
& Co. moved in when it opened in 1852.

Courtesy: California Historical Society.

England house of Adams & Co. This express company had been founded by Alvin Adams of Boston in 1840 and had become a successful business within two years. It was Haskell, a trusted clerk in the firm, who persuaded Adams to establish an office in San Francisco. He arrived in the gold-rush city on October 31, 1849, and on November 8 the company announced the opening of its San Francisco office. Here, too, the enterprise met with success and quickly became the leading express company on the Pacific Coast. In 1852 it entered the banking business, again with success. During the next few years Adams & Co. built, for its branch offices, expensive brick buildings in many California communities. They were often the most imposing structures in the towns.

Adams & Co.'s first office in San Francisco was on a lot leased from Woods. The 1850 *San Francisco Directory*, the city's first, places it on Montgomery Street between Sacramento and California streets. The structure stood on a 24½ foot section of lot 181, which Woods had purchased on November 25, 1849. It was on the east side of Montgomery, just north of the California House on California Street.[14]

There are other indications of Woods' early association with Adams & Co. Advertisements appearing in the newspapers in January 1850 gave the same address for Woods and for Adams & Co. On October 15, 1850, D.H. Haskell announced he was leaving on the *Carolina* for the East and was appointing I.C. Woods his attorney during his temporary absence.[15]

---

[14]W.D.M. Howard Papers, at the Calif. Hist. Soc. Library, San Francisco. Woods bought the property for $12,000 from Henry Teschemaker, a future mayor of San Francisco.

[15]*Alta California*, Oct. 15, 1850.

On May 4, 1851, the fifth great fire devastated San Francisco, destroying the building occupied by Adams & Co. A few days later, on May 10, Woods' uncle, Francis (Frank) Henry Woods, a clerk with Adams & Co., described the results of the fire in a letter to his mother in Maine.[16]

> A week ago tonight we were visited by a fire which laid our city in ashes... but I am pleased to say our people are not discouraged... The loss of Adams & Co. will be about five thousand dollars, but they do not care about it as they intended to have torn down the old building in about three months and put up a fire proof brick one and the fire has saved them the trouble. We shall probably have the new building ready to move into in about a month, meantime we are occupying Isaiah's warehouse for an Express Office and Banking House... I have just learnt that Isaiah's wife has made me an uncle tonight...[17]

The reference is to the birth of I.C. Woods' son Charles, born May 10, 1851.

I.C. Woods' warehouse was on a lot at the corner of Pine and Battery streets, which Woods had bought on December 11, 1849, from Joseph P. Thompson, a pioneer of 1842, for $18,000.[18] Adams & Co. occupied it only briefly, soon moving to the new building erected on the old site on Montgomery Street, as did Woods. Neither, however, stayed there long.

On December 4, 1852, John Parrott, the future banker and millionaire, opened his newly built "Granite Block," a famous landmark that for almost a hundred years stood at the northwest corner of

---

[16]F.H. Woods was born in Saco in 1819, and was associated with Adams & Co. in 1850.

[17]Letter owned by Mrs. F.H. Fallon of Santa Rosa, CA, a granddaughter of Francis (Frank) Woods.

[18]W.D.M. Howard Papers, Calif. Hist. Soc. Library, San Francisco.

Montgomery and California. The ground floor became the offices of the banking firm of Page, Bacon and Co. and also of Adams & Co. Adams leased part of the third floor as well. The flush times are indicated by Adams' rent of $1,500 a month for the ground floor space.[19] During the building's construction, Frank Woods had written to his mother that Parrott's Building "will be the most magnificent building in California." Since 1850 a Montgomery Street address had carried prestige, as indicated by the *San Francisco Picayune* reference to this street as the "Wall Street of the West,"[20] a name that remains current a hundred and thirty years later.

Sam Brannan, also a native of Saco, Maine (born in 1819, six years before Woods), in 1854 built his four-story "Express Building" on the northeast corner of Montgomery and California, next to Woods' building. Wells Fargo's headquarters was located there until the bank failures of 1855. They then moved across the street into Parrott's "Granite Block," formerly occupied by Adams & Co.

During these years I.C. Woods was listed in the directories as a "commission merchant." In 1850 he had a lumber yard at the foot of Pine Street. He also dealt in many other commodities. During that year his advertisements in the newspapers offered for sale butter, lard and other food products, a prefabricated hotel,[21] a twelve-ton schooner, and a brig named the *Cyrus*. In April 1850 he announced the sailing of the

---

[19]Barbara Donohoe Jostes, *John Parrott, Selected Papers of a Western Pioneer* (San Francisco, 1972), p. 113. The date 1851 given for the Parrott Building by A.F. Harlow in his *Old Waybills* is not correct.

[20]*San Francisco Picayune*, Sept. 11, 1850, from Kenneth Johnson, *Gleanings from the Picayune* (Georgetown, CA, 1964).

[21]*Pacific News*, Jan. 10, 1850.

ship *Canada* for the Sandwich Islands, a month later he
was advertising "the regular packet *Emily Bourne*"
leaving for Santa Cruz, Monterey, Santa Barbara, San
Pedro, and San Diego.[22] These ships carried not only
freight but also passengers. In October Woods had the
cargo of the barque *William and James* for sale.[23]

This involvement with shipping may explain the
letters written by Frank Woods, I.C. Woods' uncle but
only six years older than he. On November 23, 1850,
Frank wrote to his mother: "David [I.C. Woods'
brother] sends much love to you all. He is mate of
Isaiah's vessel and is the same old fat Dave as ever. It is a
great pity Isaiah induced him to come out here as he
was in a fair way to do well awhaling. I should think
Isaiah was doing well but I never inquire into his
business." He continued sending home news of David.
On May 27, 1851, he wrote that David "has gone down
the coast, mate of a Brig." On July 30, 1851: "David is
master of a brig belonging to Isaiah. He is the same old
David." And a few months later, on December 12,
1851, he wrote: "David and I have many a good time.
He is just like his father, generous to a fault. He is out of
employment at present."

Immediately upon his arrival in San Francisco, I.C.
Woods had not only entered into the business life of the
city but, with remarkable energy, entered also into its
civic and cultural affairs. In 1849 he helped establish
what is considered San Francisco's first public school,
joining this undertaking with Adams & Co. and such
well-known San Franciscans as Sam Brannan, Talbot
Green, and William T. Coleman.[24] On April 22, 1850,
his signature appeared among those forming the San

[22]*Alta California*, Jan. 15, 26; Feb. 20; Apr. 3, 13; May 14, 1850.
[23]*Pacific News*, Oct. 27, 1850.

Francisco Chamber of Commerce,[25] and a few months later, on September 15, he sponsored the election of Alonzo Parker for Harbor Master.[26] Also, on April 28, 1852, Woods was a sponsor of a farewell performance by Stephen Massett, a popular singer and actor who, in 1849, had given San Francisco's first theatrical performance.

Woods was prospering in business. In 1851 he was listed in *A "Pile," or A Glance at the Wealth of the Monied Men of San Francisco.* In November of that year a newspaper reported that he was traveling through the southern mining district for the benefit of Adams & Co.[27] A year later he was again in the southern mines. During this trip he met Sam Ward, who was mining without success. Ward, who later became "King of the Lobby," wrote that Woods arrived at his camp in "one of Adams and Company magnificent express wagons ...drawn by four splendid horses."[28]

In 1852 I.C. Woods was a part owner of the important but short-lived newspaper, *The San Francisco Picayune.*[29] The same year, both he and Haskell became involved in politics. In the California Whig convention, Woods was a vice-presidential elector and Haskell a presidential elector. However, the Democratic party

[24]Henry G. Langley, *The San Francisco Directory* (San Francisco, 1859), p. 30. There were several schools in San Francisco before, but all were supported by tuition. According to the 1859 annual report of the Superintendent of Schools of San Francisco, John Pelton and his wife opened the first free American common school in October 1849. John Pelton was a former principal of the Phillips' School at Andover. He arrived in California on October 11, 1849.

[25]The Articles of Incorporation state the Chamber of Commerce was established April 27, 1850, and incorporated November 3, 1851.

[26]*Alta California*, Sept. 15, 1850.

[27]*San Joaquin Republican*, Nov. 26, 1851.

[28]Carvel Collins, *Sam Ward in the Gold Rush* (Stanford, CA, 1949), p. 164.

[29]Edward C. Kemble, *A History of California Newspapers* (reprint; Los Gatos, CA, 1962), p. 107.

ADAMS & CO'S
CALIFORNIA AND ATLANTIC STATES
EXPRESS.
Office 101 Montgomery St.

Our Atlantic States Express leaves San Francisco on the 1st and 15th of each Month, by the

PACIFIC MAIL S.S. COMPANY'S
STEAMERS,

And the Treasure crosses the Isthmus under a strong Guard.

The Treasure forwarded by us to the Philadelphia Mint is always deposited there previous to that sent by any other conveyance. Our rates are *Lower* than those offered by any other House with *the same security*. We also forward Treasure, on the 1st and 15th of each month, to England, by the P. M. S. S. Co's Steamers to Panama, and from Chagres by the West India Mail Steamers.

Our small Package Express goes forward in charge of our regular special messengers, who, by constantly traveling the Isthmus, have the information and facilities not possessed by any other person. Our Express being the most extensive in the United States, we can guarantee greater facilities than can be offered by any other concern. We do a Banking Business of Deposit only, special or otherwise. We draw Bills of Exchange on any of our Houses in the following places :

Boston, New York, Philadelphia, Baltimore, Washington, St. Louis, Cincinnati, New Orleans, London, etc. etc.

In the Northern Mines we run Expresses in our own name, always accompanied by faithful Messengers, to and from the following places:

San Francisco, Benicia, Sacramento City, Marysville, Shasta, Nevada, Grass Valley, Coloma, Placerville, (or Hangtown,) Greenwood, Georgetown, Mormon Island, Salmon Falls, Auburn, and every other part of El Dorado and Placer Counties. Also, to Jackson, Dry Town, Volcano, and Sutterville, in Calaveras County. Through Langton & Co., to and from Downieville, and all other places on the Yuba and Feather Rivers. Through Cram, Rogers & Co., to Yreka, Weaverville, &c. To and from Sacramento and Stockton, via Benicia. In the Southern Mines, we run an Express in our own name, always accompanied by faithful messengers, to and from San Francisco, Stockton, Sonora, Moquelumne Hill, Columbia, Mariposa, &c. &c. By Brown's Express from Stockton to all the camps in the Southern Mines.

Our Bills of Exchange can be procured at, and Treasure forwarded to us for shipment, from any of the above places. In all of which we have Brick Vaults or Iron Safes for the security of Treasure entrusted to us, and on board of Steamboats, on any of the above routes, we have Iron Safes and Messengers for the security of all valuable Packages transported by us.

October, 1852.

BOUDOIR PORTRAIT

MORSE, PHOTO.   SAN FRANCISCO

Broadside advertisement for Adams & Co. Express.
Courtesy: Wells Fargo Bank History Department.

presidential candidate, Franklin Pierce, carried
California. Also in 1854 Haskell served as a San
Francisco supervisor.

Throughout 1853 Woods continued to participate in
the affairs of his adopted city and state. One of the most
desired, most popular projects of Californians was the
building of a transcontinental railroad which would
end their isolation, uniting them with the East most
had so recently left, and I.C. Woods might have
become the head of the first rail system to cross the
nation. In the autumn of 1853, at a meeting attended by
leading San Franciscans, the Atlantic and Pacific
Railroad Company was organized. Haskell became a
vice-president. The next year Woods became one of its
four sponsors, with Thomas Larkin, Captain Joseph
Folsom, and Colonel Edward Baker. On January 3,
1855, he was elected a director, and on January 11 he
became president. All of this activity came to a halt,
however, after the financial collapse that occurred a few
weeks later, and ultimately it was a group of
Sacramento merchants, not the financial leaders of San
Francisco, who built the transcontinental railroad. To
Leland Stanford, not Woods, went the honor of
heading it.

His political interests had led Woods into a
controversy of some bitterness in 1853. David
Broderick and his followers in the State Legislature
tried to pass an act known as the Extension Bill. It
stipulated that the San Francisco waterfront would be
extended six hundred feet into San Francisco Bay
beyond the line fixed by law in 1851 as the permanent
waterfront. It would have enriched those who had
water lots in the Bay, which included Broderick, but
hurt those with property in the established waterfront

sections of the city. Woods joined other well-known citizens in defeating this scheme, which the daily *Herald* labeled "knavery" and the historian John Hittell called "one of the great frauds."[30] The same year, 1853, he was elected a member of the prestigious Society of California Pioneers.

Adams & Co. became the largest express organization on the Pacific Coast. It bought or merged with other express companies: Ballou's, Hardin's, Freeman's, Newell's, among them. It was praised by the *Alta California* in an article on September 18, 1853, which pointed out that it had "relays of the finest horses" and that its "riders were picked men. . . daring and dauntless." According to A.L. Stimson in his history of express companies, Adams even initiated a pony express system.[31]

By 1853 Adams & Co. was generally regarded as California's leading business organization. It handled more money, dealt with more people, and furnished more services to industry and commerce than any other.[32]

In May 1854 D.H. Haskell returned to San Francisco from the East and announced that the ownership of the Pacific Coast firm had been altered.[33] It now consisted of Haskell himself and Woods as general partners; Alvin Adams of Boston, founder of the original firm, became only a "special partner." I.C. Woods became president, while Adams remained head

[30]John S. Hittell, *A History of the City of San Francisco* (San Francisco, 1878), pp. 313-16.

[31]A.L. Stimson, *History of the Express Business* (New York, 1881).

[32]Hittell, *History of San Francisco*, p. 228.

[33]The dissolved firm consisted of Alvin Adams of Boston, William B. Dinsmore of New York, D.H. Haskell of San Francisco, and E.S. Sanford and I.M. Shoemaker.

Alvin Adams started his famous Express in Boston in 1840. It soon
became successful and during the Civil War
made enormous profits.

of the Adams & Co. in the East. Alvin Adams'
connection as a "special partner" led to much
controversy after the Pacific Coast Adams & Co. failed.
Adams claimed he had no financial connection with
the western firm and refused to pay any of the claims.
Neill Wilson, in his 1936 interpretive history of Wells,
Fargo & Company, described Woods' advancement in
these words: "Isaiah Woods, who had ceased to be
Adams' landlord,... was the driver seemingly born to
handle the wild horses of their chariot of commerce."[34]

At the time of the change, however, a different view
of I.C. Woods' standing was given by Frank Woods in
another letter to his mother in Boston:[35]

> By the House of Adams and Co. at home [in the East] he is
> looked upon as a consumate scoundrel... Mr. Adams came
> out here with the express purpose of discharging him but the
> old man was so delighted with the country that he was almost
> beside himself and Woods and Haskell took good care to
> keep it up and from morning until night they kept him
> agoing on a continual round of pleasure, so that he had no
> time to look at accounts and went home as wise as he came...
> Mr. Bowers from the Boston office... called on me... he
> said he had known for three years Woods was one of the
> biggest rascals in California.

He wrote that I.C. Woods had discharged him from
Adams & Co. after four years of "faithful service," and
he bitterly accused his nephew of being "a thief and a
rascal... getting rich off the House rapidly."[36]

A paragraph in a biography of Alvin Adams written
three years after his death corroborates part of Frank
Woods' statement. It appeared in the October 1877
issue of *The Expressman's Monthly:*

[34]Neill Wilson, *Treasure Express* (New York, 1936), p. 70.
[35]Letter in the collection of Mrs. Virginia Fallon, dated Apr. 30, 1854.
[36]*Ibid.*

When the California fever broke out in 1849, Mr. Adams
was first in the field... After the express had been doing
finely, in an evil day they opened a bank. When Mr. Adams
went to San Francisco the whole town rose at him. He went
to inspect, but he had no time for that. He was wined all day
and dined at night. He was carried from point to point in a
carriage drawn by four horses, and treated like a prince.
When he got back he said he didn't know whether he was
Alvin Adams or the Great Mogul. At all events he knew he
hadn't done what he went to do.

Frank Woods' view of his nephew was colored by
personal factors. His letters indicate that I.C. Woods
had not been cordial to him for a long time. On July 30,
1853, Frank wrote to his sister. "I have not seen I.C.
Woods for four months. Some times I meet him in the
streets. He only passes the time of the day and that very
coldly. He never comes to see me, but I do not care for
that."[37]

His discharge from Adams & Co. did not prevent
Frank from living a long and honorable life. He
remained in San Francisco until his death on July 8,
1900, at his Nob Hill residence at 913 Pine Street. He
had long been a member of the San Francisco Stock
Exchange, elected in October 1863, one year after its
formation. He accumulated a large amount of San
Francisco property, and he was listed in the city's
earliest society directories. A son, Harry F. Woods,
inherited from him a "handsome fortune."[38]

While I.C. Woods may have been under suspicion
by some, as indicated in Frank's 1854 letter, he
continued an active and to all appearances a blameless
life in California. One of his ventures was planning the

---

[37]Letter in the collection of Mrs. Virginia Fallon.
[38]Information from his obituary in the *San Francisco Chronicle*, July 10, 1900, and
from Mrs. Fallon.

town of Ravenswood in the southern part of San Francisco County, the part which, in 1856, became San Mateo County. The site is near the present city of Menlo Park. In the early 1850s many towns were planned and promoted in California. Colonel J.D. Stevenson envisioned the "City of New York of the Pacific," already mentioned; John Bidwell and Lansford Hastings laid out Sutterville, now within the city limits of Sacramento; A.J. Grayson planned a town in Stanislaus County to bear his name. All, like Ravenswood, were dreams that failed.

Woods' interest in developing Ravenswood may have had its origin in the Atlantic and Pacific Railroad scheme, for the line was to go through this town. But in addition, the site of Ravenswood was well located on San Francisco Bay, and water transportation was still the main means of travel, as roads were few and poor. Only a short wharf from solid dry land would be needed to reach deep water. The future of the town appeared bright, as it was near the lumber mills in the hills, which were sending wood for construction of the "instant city" of San Francisco. Potentially rich farming land was nearby as well.[39] A railroad bridge which would cross the bay from Alameda County to Ravenswood was envisioned. However, it was not until 1925 that this crossing was accomplished with the construction of the Dumbarton Bridge.[40]

Ravenswood was to be located on land which I.C.

---

[39] Frank Stanger, *La Peninsula*, vol. 8, no. 5 (San Mateo, 1946).

[40] After the completion of the transcontinental railroad in 1869, a bridge at this site was again considered. However, the *San Francisco Chronicle*, Dec. 1871, reported the bridge to Ravenswood would probably not be built as the cost would be $3,000,000. Earlier, in 1863, the first railroad from San Francisco to San Jose ran through Redwood City, the former Mezesville, and not through Ravenswood.

Woods had bought in 1852. It was part of the Rancho de las Pulgas, which had been granted to Luis Antonio Argüello in 1824 and 1835. On July 23, 1852, Woods had acquired about 2,000 acres, much of it in the present Menlo Park. In 1853 he conveyed one half of his acreage to Haskell. However, the following year Haskell conveyed all his land back to Woods, who then commenced the town's development. The site was bordered roughly by San Francisco Bay, what is now Middlefield Road (then called Middle Road), and Willow and Marsh Roads.[41]

On this property Woods created a country estate for himself which he named Woodside Dairy (not to be confused with the present town of Woodside); like "Ravenswood," the name contained his own. Woods' location of his estate in this area was said in a 1916 history of the county to have initiated Menlo Park's development as a region of country seats of wealthy gentlemen. This history indicated that the Woodside Dairy residence was superior to any in the vicinity at that time, and Woods made it a "scene of many delightful entertainments." His guests traveled by steamer down the bay to the Ravenswood dock to be met by carriage and driven to his home.[42]

Woods had the town surveyed and streets laid out. Many of the street names recall well-known San Franciscans: Dore, Nugent, Garrison, Bowie, Brannan, Vioget, Argüello, and Folsom. There was also a Haskell Street and a Woods Street, as well as a Charles Street, probably named for Woods' son.[43]

---

[41]John T. Doyle, pamphlet regarding the title to his land, 1889.

[42]Philip W. Alexander and Charles P. Hamm, *History of San Mateo County* (Burlingame, CA, 1916), p. 51.

[43]Map of the town of Ravenswood, Recorder's Office, San Francisco City Hall.

After the failure of Adams & Co. in 1855, the dream of the city of Ravenswood faded away, as did many other California dreams. However, it had the distinction of being the site of San Mateo County's first town. Only its name still exists: Ravenswood Street in Menlo Park, and Ravenswood School District in nearby East Palo Alto.

Early in 1854 Adams & Co. built the large North Point Dock Warehouse (later known as the Seawall Warehouse) in San Francisco. It was a two-story brick building at Sansome and Lombard streets, on a fifty-vara lot cut from Telegraph Hill.[44] When completed, it was leased to Woods' close friend A.A. Cohen, a native of England who arrived in California in 1849.[45] He was to be an associate of I.C. Woods for many years.

In October 1854 California held its first State Fair, sponsored by the State Agricultural Society. Since 1861 the State Fair has been held in Sacramento; previously it was held in various cities. The first was held in San Francisco at the Musical Hall, built by Henry ("Honest Harry") Meiggs in 1853 on Bush Street near Montgomery; the site is now marked by an official state plaque. However, the cattle, horses, etc., were exhibited at the Pioneer Race Track, bounded by Mission, Bryant, 24th, and Army streets in the Mission District.

The *San Francisco Herald* reported on October 6 that Adams & Co.'s display of specimens of wheat "from each county in the state gives an opportunity of

---

[44]*San Francisco Alta*, Jan. 7, 1854. Later this warehouse was rented to William T. Coleman. In 1868 John Ziele became the owner, and his family retained the historic building until shortly before its demolition in 1968.

[45]A.A. Cohen married Emilie Gibbons, daughter of Dr. Henry Gibbons, in 1854.

comparing the fertility of various sections of the country." The article continued that "Mr. I.C. Woods has some specimens on exhibit, which will, we believe, be among that destined to receive the greatest consideration of the committee."

Woods also exhibited at the Pioneer Race Track. Listed were his "Stallion Peacock, imported from Kentucky in 1852,"[46] a "colt sired by Peacock, a breeding mare Lady Spear, an iron grey gelding, 28 months, a gray filly from General Vallejo's Andalusia, out of Lady Spear, and a bay colt, sired by Peacock out of Lady Spear." Also Woods showed a pair of bay road horses, Flying Dick and Cock Robin, all of the which indicates the affluence of I.C. Woods in 1854.

San Francisco was changing. California had increased its agriculture, so the city's port became less active in receiving foodstuffs from the East.[47] Placer mining had become less successful. For the most part, the days were virtually over when an individual miner with pick and pan could strike it rich. Crowds of disenchanted miners were drifting into San Francisco, changing the labor market. The financial stability of the city was given a severe blow in October 1854 when it was disclosed that when Henry Meiggs, a leading citizen and a member of the Board of Aldermen, and his brother John, the City Controller, had forged several hundred thousand dollars in city warrants. Adams & Co.'s loss was $40,000. Following Meiggs' flight from the city, the Grand Jury indicted Hamilton Bowie, the City Treasurer. I.C. Woods was called as a witness, but

[46]The good repute of "Peacock" is shown in a suit in 1867 brought by George Gordon to regain a mare sired by "Peacock," the mare being highly valued because of her breeding.

[47]Hittell, *History of San Francisco*, pp. 215-17.

he refused to testify, claiming "all business transactions are sacred."[48]

Although there were signs of an oncoming commercial depression, Woods was apparently prosperous and continued his usual activities. One was sponsorship of an ambitious stage line project. He joined with R.E. Doyle, John T. Doyle, Eugene Casserly, and James Birch, president of the California Stage Company, to form the Emigrant Route Company. They urged the state to grant them a one million dollar contract for a line of stages to run from Missouri to Salt Lake, then follow the Humboldt River to the Carson Valley, and end in Sacramento.

In spite of indications of trouble in financial affairs in California in 1854, the year ended with Adams & Co. holding its place as a leading banking institution and the largest express company on the Pacific Coast.

---

[48]*San Francisco Alta*, Mar. 15, 1855, reported Bowie was found "not guilty." Bowie was a brother of Dr. Augustus J. Bowie. Hamilton Bowie died late in 1856 in Nicaragua with Walker's filibusters.

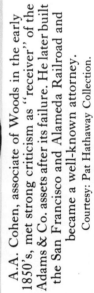

A.A. Cohen, associate of Woods in the early 1850's, met strong criticism as "receiver" of the Adams & Co. assets after its failure. He later built the San Francisco and Alameda Railroad and became a well-known attorney.

Courtesy: Pat Hathaway Collection.

James King of William was associated with Adams & Co. at the time of its closing. Founder of the *Bulletin*, he became Woods' enemy. His death, by the gun of Casey, led to the formation of the Vigilance Committee of 1856.

Courtesy: Bancroft Library.

II

Failure

The year 1855 was disastrous for San Francisco and for I.C. Woods. In spite of signs in 1854 that the boom years were over, as 1855 began, Adams & Co. did not appear concerned about the dark clouds forming. It sent Fred Cohen, brother of Woods' confidant A.A. Cohen, to visit its offices in northern California. He examined the books at Mud Springs, Diamond Springs,[1] and Coloma and suggested that the agent in Coloma be replaced. He continued on to Placer County, visiting Iowa Hill, Yankee Jims, and Auburn, then went to Downieville in Sierra County. There he arranged to purchase the express line of Samuel Langton. The sale was not completed,[2] however, for two days later Adams & Co. collapsed.

All had been peaceful in San Francisco's banking world in January and early February. Then on February 17, 1855, the S.S. *Oregon* arrived from Panama with news that the banking house of Page, Bacon and Company in St. Louis had suspended. It was catastrophic news for the San Francisco office of Page, Bacon, and ultimately catastrophic for Adams & Co.

---

[1]Mud Springs (later named El Dorado) and Diamond Springs were near Placerville in El Dorado County.

[2]Langton never entirely recovered financially. However, he continued to operate until his accidental death in 1864. Soon afterwards his lines were absorbed by Wells, Fargo (M.C. Nathan, *Franks of Western Expresses* [Chicago, 1973], pp. 126-28).

The St. Louis firm had become involved in the construction of a railroad between Cincinnati and St. Louis, an expensive venture. A New York bank which had agreed to assist it suddenly refused to do so, and Page, Bacon suspended.[3]

An observer vividly described the events of that February morning when the *Oregon* brought the bad news. At 8:30 a.m. the employees of Page, Bacon were sitting around the offices of the bank joking; at 9:05, just after the arrival of the ship, about six men came into the bank to make withdrawals. Twenty-five minutes later a whole crowd of depositors "of the lower class" filled the office clamoring for their funds. Immediately all were paid in full.

The leading merchants held a meeting later that day urging everyone to be calm. Woods was among those who spoke; he stated that Page, Bacon was "sound." The newspapers also attempted to allay the people's fears. For example, the *San Francisco Chronicle* stated Page, Bacon and Company would pay all its obligations, that its vaults contained over a million dollars. However, the reassurances were of no avail. When the offices of Page, Bacon and Company opened on the second day, they were soon filled with "women shrieking and crying" and "men swearing and

---

[3]The St. Louis bank had been established by Daniel D. Page, who, with his son-in-law Henry D. Bacon, was in charge of the parent office. Francis W. Page, son of Daniel, was in charge of the Sacramento office. Daniel Page's daughter Carrie was married to William T. Coleman. Henry Haight was manager of the San Francisco office.

A rumor had previously been reported regarding the financial credit of "the great house of Page, Bacon of St. Louis." The *San Francisco Chronicle* on August 14, 1854, stated that the rumor claimed the house was in difficulties because of its railroad contracts. This the newspaper denied, claiming not only was the report false but that "Page, Bacon & Co. of this city have no connection whatever with them and is no way affected by it." Both the *San Francisco Herald* and the *San Francisco Daily Placer Times and Transcript*, on the same date, called the rumor "groundless."

yelling."[4] In the next few days $800,000 in gold was paid out. Then, on February 22, Page, Bacon and Company suspended payment.[5]

Later that same day Adams & Co. closed its San Francisco office after paying out $200,000 in gold.[6] As mentioned, both Page, Bacon's and Adams & Co.'s San Francisco offices were located in Parrott's Granite Block, and many believed there was a business relationship between them.

Runs on other banks forced them also to close that same day, which has gone down in San Francisco history as "Black Friday."[7] A.S. Wright's Miner Exchange, Robinson and Co., Sanders and Brenham, Burgoyne and Company, and Argenti and Company all closed. Lucas, Turner and Company,[8] Drexel, Sather and Church, B. Davidson (agent for the Rothschilds), and Palmer, Cook and Co. survived. Palmer and Cook did not have a run, as it received the government tax money and was known to have a large sum on hand. Wells, Fargo & Company shut its doors but opened again three days later. Nevertheless, the panic continued.

It spread rapidly through the interior. A crowd of miners flocked into Grass Valley from the surrounding diggings and threatened to break into the Adams & Co. banks. At Auburn an armed crowd compelled the Adams agent to open the vault and distribute the gold.

[4]Letter at the History Department, Wells Fargo Bank, San Francisco.

[5]Dwight L. Clarke, *William Tecumseh Sherman, Gold Rush Banker* (San Francisco, 1969), p. 112.

[6]*Ibid.* H.H. Bancroft wrote: "When this institution [Adams'] fell, faith in banks seemed for a time destroyed" *(Works, History of California,* vol. 7 [San Francisco, 1890]. p. 174).

[7]Ira Cross, *Financing an Empire,* vol. 1 (Chicago, San Francisco, and Los Angeles, 1927), p. 183.

[8]*Ibid.,* p. 169.

In Columbia and Sonora mobs formed. In the latter, the mob stormed the Adams office and dispensed the gold in a haphazard manner. There were similar panics elsewhere.[9]

A Plumas County miner, George Tufly, described the resulting situation in many mining communities. "Business bad," he wrote on April 10, 1855, "winter dry and miners had no water with which to work. Another reason is the unheard of loss of peoples' savings through the bankruptcy of Adams & Co. The loss amounts to six million dollars which makes money around here very scarce because the miners had invested their last cent."[10]

In San Francisco alone, two hundred business firms failed that year. A major factor in this financial disaster was lack of communication with the East. There was yet no transcontinental telegraph; the fastest way for news to travel was by sea, on ships that took three to four weeks. Had the S.S. *Oregon* not been several days late, the panic might have been averted. On the 16th, the day before the *Oregon* entered the Golden Gate, the S.S. *Golden Age* had left for Panama with a shipment of $1,287,364 in gold from the banks, most of it from Page, Bacon and Co. and Adams & Co. If the *Oregon* had arrived on time, the gold would have been held and the run on Page, Bacon and Co. might have been managed.

After Adams and Co. closed on "Black Friday," a long meeting was held in attorney John T. Doyle's office. It lasted most of the night. Woods' friend A.A. Cohen was selected as the company's "assignee," receiver, with instructions to take charge of all assets.

---

[9]Alvin F. Harlow, *Old Waybills* (New York, 1934), p. 164.

[10]George Tufly wrote to his brother in Illinois. *Pony Express*, Oct. 1950, p. 7.

During this meeting there was a heated argument over whether or not the firm should re-open and attempt to pay with gold dust, of which Adams & Co. had a large supply. Trenor W. Park, the attorney for the firm, insisted that to do so would be hazardous, and his view prevailed.[11] The same night Cohen, acting on advice of counsel, moved the remaining gold to the firm of Alsop and Co. for safety, as mob action was feared. This gold was later deposited with the banking firm of Palmer and Cook.

Two days after the closing, on February 24, Adams & Co. announced that its liabilities would be paid from its assets. Following the announcement Woods issued a broadside describing at length the reasons for the closing of the company and blaming others for the firm's difficulties. He claimed that in spite of his "repeated inquiries... our house received always the assurance of the perfect ability of Page, Bacon and Co. to meet any run... Therefore ... we did not concentrate our resources here from all parts of the State." He asked that the creditors allow Adams & Co. to stay open, promising that they could pay 25% in thirty days and the remainder as soon as possible. This was not accepted by the public. Judging from what occurred, it appears unfortunate that Woods' plan was not given a chance.

On February 26 Cohen wrote a letter to Alvin Adams explaining it was his "painful duty" to report that they were "compelled to suspend," owing to the closing of Page, Bacon and Company and Adams' paucity of coin. Cohen assured Adams they had over $1,200,000 in assets, which would meet all debts.[12]

[11]Bancroft, *History of California*, vol. 7, p. 175.
[12]Letter at the Huntington Library, San Marino, CA.

John T. Doyle was Woods' confidant. An eminent attorney and early president of the California Historical Society, his brother (R.E. Doyle) married Woods' sister.

Courtesy: Society of California Pioneers.

Treanor Park, Woods' foe, was attorney for Adams & Co. at its failure in 1855. In the 1860's he returned east, becoming enormously wealthy in transportation enterprises, including the Panama Railroad.

Courtesy: California Historical Society.

However, two days later I.C. Woods filed a petition of insolvency in Adams & Co.'s name, bringing California's largest express company to an inglorious end.[13]

Letters on February 25 and 28, 1855, to Faxon Atherton in Valparaiso from his agent in San Francisco, Alexander Grogan, reflect opinions typical at this time. Grogan described the closing of the banks and charged that the partners of Adams & Co. had been "living in the style of princes for a long time." He also questioned the conduct of the partners, claiming they had "taken care to secure themselves and their friends with funds of the concern," a belief which was not true, as later events showed. Grogan also wrote that the depositors in the main were people of little means, declaring that in the closing of Adams & Co. "the poor are the greatest sufferers."[14]

Cohen, as receiver, had many problems. Property owned by the bank was attached, so that he could not sell it. Because of the statewide depression, costly buildings erected by Adams & Co. had to be disposed of at only a fraction of their true value. Cohen's attempts to have the funds sent to him from the branches in the interior met with only partial success. As already mentioned, mobs had prevailed in some towns.

Attempts to settle matters continued. Cohen filed suit against the company's attorneys, Trenor W. Park and Frederick Billings. He claimed Park had collected a $10,000 fee for legal work from Adams & Co. the evening before the firm's suspension; Cohen wanted this returned. This suit against such a prestigious law firm as Park, Halleck, Peachy and Billings gave rise to

[13]*California Chronicle*, Feb. 28, 1855.
[14]Letters at the Calif. Hist. Soc.

much bitterness, which continued for years. Park and Billings responded to Cohen with "cards" in the San Francisco newspapers denying all charges. On March 19, 1855, Park was arrested,[15] but the charges were never pressed. Later in March, Park, representing Alvin Adams, sued both Woods and Haskell for alleged fraud.[16] In June, Halleck, Peachy and Billings brought suit against Cohen, also alleging fraud. As was the custom, Cohen replied in the papers, claiming the charges were false and "known to be false" by the attorneys.

The depositors of Adams & Co. had called a mass meeting, elected officers, and suggested that three assignees be named. On April 9, Judge Delos Lake renamed Cohen and added Richard Roman and Edward Jones, the latter with Palmer, Cook and Company.

A letter from a depositor in the Adams bank appeared in the newspapers in June charging that Alvin Adams and the eastern company were liable for the debts of the western Adams & Co. Many were of this opinion, but it was never upheld by the courts.

The assignees had urged a pro-rate distribution of the funds of Adams & Co., but on July 13 the court ruled that only certain specific claims by individuls were to be paid. The assignees claimed this aided a "few active and shrewd speculators" who "bought up certificates at low cost." Among those named as large holders were A.A. Selover, auctioneer, and Joseph Palmer of Palmer, Cook and Company. On the same day, Cohen accused Park of "professional treachery," and Woods in an affidavit stated that Billings and Park, when attorneys

[15]*San Francisco Herald*, Mar. 14, 16, 19, 1855.
[16]*San Francisco Herald*, Mar. 24, 1855.

for Adams & Co. just after the suspension of the firm, started an "amenable suit" with Adams & Co.'s permission, a suit that had developed into quite the opposite.

A more serious charge was leveled by Page, Bacon and Company when they filed suit in the Twelfth District Court against I.C. Woods and A.A. Cohen charging them with selling their bank gold dust of inferior quality. The complainants stated in an affidavit that gold dust from the northern mines, worth $7.25 an ounce, was altered by a chemical process and sold to them as gold dust from the southern mines for $14.50 an ounce. Page, Bacon and Company claimed they had lost $400,000 by this fraud.[17] Woods and Cohen were arrested. Cohen posted bail, but Woods refused and was jailed. On July 18 Judge Edward Norton of the Twelfth District Court, who had replaced Lake, discharged both Cohen and Woods on the grounds that the affidavit "was a mere matter of personal belief." However, the accusation was again in the news in August when the *Weekly Chronicle* reported that the machinery for making bogus gold of the finest quality had been found and that it belonged to I.C. Woods.[18]

On July 13 there was more excitement. Frederick Cohen, the former Adams & Co. agent, was arrested and fined $300 for attacking Trenor Park, whom he claimed had made derogatory remarks about his brother, A.A. Cohen.

Meanwhile, I.C. Woods had been shorn of much of his property. His San Francisco house on Stockton Street, a "large brick home" where he lived with his

[17]*Alta California*, July 12, 1855. Francis Page wrote in his diary (at the Calif. Hist. Soc.) that he believed the truth of the charges.

[18]*San Francisco Weekly Chronicle*, Aug. 11, 1855.

mother, sister, wife, and son, was sold by the sheriff.[19]
The sheriff also sold Woods' part of the Rancho de las
Pulgas, including the site of Ravenswood. A large
portion was bought by the brothers John T. and Robert
Emmett Doyle and their brother-in-law, Eugene
Casserly. Robert Emmett Doyle lived for many years in
the home Woods had built there.[20] Casserly's part of
the property later became the Joseph Donahoe estate.

Woods was apparently unable to continue facing his
problems on their home ground. On August 7, 1855, he
left San Francisco secretly, sailing on the bark *Audubon*
for Australia, a flight reminiscent of Henry Meiggs'
the previous year. Aboard ship, Woods wrote to Cohen
explaining his sudden departure.[21] He had attended
the wedding ceremony of his sister Sarah to Robert
Emmett Doyle, he explained.[22] He was expected to
follow them to the ranch for a wedding supper in the
afternoon. Instead, he boarded the ship with his wife
and his son, Charlie. Woods informed Cohen he was
bound for Sydney but would continue on to London. In
the letter Woods referred to Trenor Park in bitter
terms, accusing him of "treachery."

There was also a second letter to Cohen informing
him of Woods' departure written by A.E. Richardson,
who had been an Adams & Co. agent. It was written, at
Woods' request, ten days after his departure.
Richardson wrote Cohen that Woods was taking a
"circuitous route to avoid his persecutors." He
continued that when Park discovered that Woods was
on his way to New York, he would "undoubtedly

[19]Clarke, *William Tecumseh Sherman*, p. 121.
[20]R.E. Doyle sold his estate in 1875.
[21]Letter at the Huntington Library.
[22]Sarah Woods and R.E. Doyle were marreid by Archbishop Sadoc Alemany.

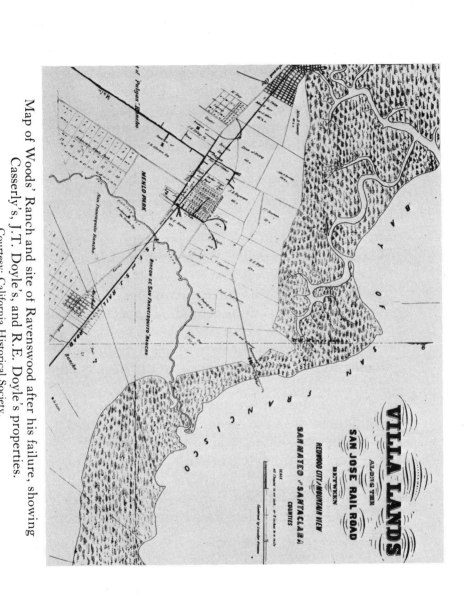

Map of Woods' Ranch and site of Ravenswood after his failure, showing Casserly's, J.T. Doyle's, and R.E. Doyle's properties.
Courtesy: California Historical Society.

trump up more charges ... [and] if possible have him arrested in New York and then returned to San Francisco." Richardson also told of dissolution of the partnership of Park, Halleck, Peachy and Billings, with Park leaving to form a partnership with Judge O.C. Shafter, noting that Park "still continues trying his cases in the newspapers," and concluding, "All's well that ends well! Every dog must have its day... if Park is not hung, law will be cheated of its due."[23]

In recent years reports have appeared in various histories of Ravenswood about I.C. Woods' being forced at gun point to yield a large sum of gold at his Woodside Dairy estate. A creditor of Adams & Co., "Maurice Dooley," is said to have obtained $80,000 of hidden gold. There are no contemporary reports of this incident; however, none would be expected. Dooley's action was illegal, since all gold was ordered placed with the receiver for the benefit of all creditors. Thus if Dooley told of this incident, it would have been years later.[24]

If Woods did remove any gold from Adams & Co., it would have to have been before February 22; and conveying $80,000 in gold to his country estate would have been extremely difficult. In any case, from Woods' letters and his actions after his flight, it is evident that he left San Francisco carrying little gold.

A.A. Cohen also left San Francisco, but with the

[23]Letter at the Huntington Library.

[24]The *San Francisco Directory of 1854* listed a "Morris Dooley," an expressman with the express firm of Dillon, Hedge and Co., located on Kearny near Merchant in San Francisco. This firm appears to have become Gilbert and Hedge and in 1859 was associated with the better-known G.H. Wines' Atlantic, California and Oregon Express.

Tinkham, in his *History of Stockton*, wrote in 1880 that a "Maurice Dooly" obtained the stage and express line of Fisher & Co. around 1864 and that Stockton line ran until about 1869.

court's permission to be away for three months. He and
his family departed on July 31 on the S.S. *Golden Age* for
New York, sailing under the assumed name of
Goodenough.[25] On October 1, during his absence, he
was replaced as receiver of Adams & Co. by Henry M.
Naglee.[26]

When he returned on November 14, Cohen was
asked by Naglee to deliver to him all the money and
records of Adams & Co. Judge John Hager, of the
Fourth Judicial District ordered Cohen to comply.
Both Cohen and another of the three appointed
assignees, Edward Jones, refused and were found guilty
of contempt. However, in December Judge T.W.
Freelon ordered them discharged.

Two months after Woods had departed, a former
associate in Adams & Co., James King of William,
established a daily newspaper, the *San Francisco
Bulletin*, which launched a continuing flow of attacks
upon many San Francisco institutions, among them
banks and bankers.[27] Woods, A.A. Cohen, and their
attorneys were among King's favorite targets. Woods
was labeled "the most consumate scoundrel this state
has ever harbored," and the paper called him Palmer,

[25]"Correspondent" letter to the *Alta*, dated Aug. 13, published Sept. 3, 1855.

[26]Henry Morris Naglee (1815-1886), a Texan by birth, was a graduate of West
Point and served in the Mexican War. In 1849, with Richard Sinton, he
established one of the first San Francisco banks. There is a monument in his honor
in St. James Park, San Jose, where he had an estate.

[27]King started his newspaper in October 1855; it was increased in size on
November 5 and again on November 30. On January 18, 1856, it achieved the
regular size of that time. In 1858 Kemble wrote: "His paper took like fire runs"
(Edward C. Kemble, *A History of California Newspapers, 1846-1858* [reprint, Los
Gatos, CA, 1962], p. 122).

King's anti-Irish, anti-Catholic attitude is shown in his remarks about Woods'
intimates. The American-born college graduate John T. Doyle is referred to as
"O'Doyle" speaking with a brogue, while Casserly is noted for his "Jesuitical
cunning."

Cook & Company's "friend and protege" in its vitriolic
attacks upon that company.[28]

A rival newspaper, the *California Chronicle*, expressed
the view of some when its editor addressed King with
the accusation that "you took and gnawed the bone
given you by I.C. Woods, and the moment he was
powerless, you turned like a cur and bit the hand which
had saved you from ruin."[29]

The reference was to King's initial association with
Woods in 1854, when a bank which King owned failed
and Woods took him into Adams & Co. Woods
arranged for Adams & Co. to take over King's assets
and assume his liabilities and to hire King at $1,000 a
month. The assets included King's three-story bank
building[30] and his considerable interest in the
Tuolumne Hydraulic Canal. Mining canal companies
were considered potential sources of wealth by
investors in the 1850s; this one, like the Mokelumne
Hill Canal and Mining Company, which Woods
himself invested in,[31] proved costly and in the end
unsuccessful financially. King had been a director of
the Tuolumne Hydraulic Canal since 1852. The sixty-
mile canal was one of the longest in the state and also
one of the most costly at that time, requiring an outlay
of $300,000.

King had another connection with Adams & Co.,
one that J. Ross Browne, United States Special

[28]*San Francisco Daily Bulletin*, Jan. 30, 1856.

[29]William L. Newell, *California Chronicle*, Nov. 5, 1855.

[30]A plaque on the present building at the southwest corner of Montgomery and
Commercial streets marks the site of King's bank.

[31]Stock certificates of Woods in the author's possession. This company was
established by Henry Eno (W. Turrentine Jackson, *Twenty Years on the Pacific
Slope: Letters of Henry Eno from California and Nevada, 1848-1871* [New Haven,
1965]. pp. 47-64).

Agent,[32] reported as improper. King and Adams & Co. obtained a contract with Lewis A. Birdsall, Superintendent of the San Francisco Mint (and father-in-law of the future governor and U.S. Senator Milton Latham), and Agoston Haraszthy (the future "Father of California's Viticulture") to form a private gold-refining firm. Their contract was termed a "federal scandal" and was short-lived.

James King, when he became associated with Adams & Co., wrote a letter to his bank's depositors informing them that as of June 27, 1854, he would be "in charge of the Banking Department of the firm of Adams & Co." and that he trusted "the same confidence will be extended to the house" which he had become "associated with."[33] He continued working for Adams & Co. until the Adams closure on Black Friday.

The *San Francisco Bulletin*, which he established in October 1855, eight months after the fall of Adams & Co., was widely criticized as a destroyer of personal reputations. Henry Gibbons, the eminent physician, did not exaggerate greatly when he wrote of King, "he made a business of murdering the reputations of all who crossed his path."[34]

Although Woods had left San Francisco, litigation involving him as well as the others connected with

---

[32]J. Ross Browne, the noted Irish-born writer and humorist, was the official reporter of California's Constitutional Convention in 1849. In 1854 he was a United States Special Agent for the Treasury Department, investigating federal affairs on the Pacific Coast. Later he was Commissioner of Mines and Mining and finally United States Minister to China. See Richard H. Dillon, *J. Ross Browne, Confidential Agent in California* (Norman, OK, 1965) and David M. Goodman, *A Western Panorama. . .* J. Ross Browne (Glendale, CA, 1966); also Brian McGinly, *Haraszthy at the Mint* (Los Angeles, 1975), pp. 26-27.

[33]Letter at the Wells Fargo Bank History Department.

[34]Letter published in Henry Harris, M.D., *California's Medical Story* (San Francisco, 1932), p. 353.

Adams & Co. continued. A suit was filed by Edward
Stanly[35], representing Alvin Adams, against Woods
and Haskell. Eugene Casserly, as counsel for the
defendants, submitted a ten-page printed brief,
declaring there was no basis for bringing suit.[36] A.A.
Cohen, becoming alarmed at the public outcry
reflected in the *Bulletin's* stories, attempted to leave San
Francisco on the S.S. *Uncle Sam* on January 6, 1856.
The authorities had been informed, however, and the
ship was searched. Cohen was found and briefly
jailed.[37] The same day, his brother, Fred Cohen, again
became incensed, this time over the wording of a
placard on the *Bulletin's* wall. He tore it off and threw it
through a window of the newspaper's office. For this he
was again arrested.[38]

Meanwhile, A.A. Cohen continued to withhold the
Adams & Co. papers from Henry M. Naglee, and on
January 28, 1856, he was found in contempt, fined
$500, and again ordered to deliver the account books.
He still refused. Naglee then took Cohen to court,
charging him with embezzlement. Through his
attorney, Naglee accused Cohen of receiving "very
large amounts of coin, gold dust and bullion for which
he had given no account," $400,000 worth. In
addition, there was the sum of one million dollars that
Cohen had claimed Adams & Co. had in assets that had
disappeared. Alvin Adams was a party to the suit,
represented at that time by his attorney Trenor Park.

[35]Edward Stanly was the Republican nominee for governor of California in 1857;
he was defeated by John Weller. Stanly was married to a sister of California
Supreme Court Justice Joseph Baldwin.

[36]Pamphlet, *Alvin Adams vs. Isaiah C. Woods and Daniel H. Haskell in the matter of
the petition of Edward Stanly.*

[37]*Alta California,* Jan. 6, 1856.

[38]*Alta California,* Jan. 8, 1856.

The trial was lengthy, involved, and acrimonious. Edward Stanly, who was Naglee's attorney as well as Alvin Adams', charged Woods and Cohen with illegal dealings in connection with their association with the two-year-old California Steam Navigation Company.[39] He also quoted from letters which he alleged showed that Cohen and Woods dealt in bogus gold dust. Most damaging to Cohen was the sensational discovery of the missing Adams & Co. account books. They were recovered by fishermen in the Bay near the North Point warehouse which, as has been mentioned, was leased to A.A. Cohen. However, the important pages of February 21 and 22, 1855, "Black Friday" and the preceding day, were missing!

Trenor Park's accusations were even more potentially damaging than Stanly's. Park claimed the belligerent Fred Cohen had thrown the Adams & Co. books in the Bay after the commencement of this trial. Park also verbally attacked Colonel E.D. Baker, Cohen's counsel.[40] "Look at his face," Park said, "and say if you do not see unmistakable evidence of indulgence in vice? Who are his associates?... Look in the gambling hells of the city."[41]

The bitter month-long trial came to an end on March

[39]The California Steam Navigation Company, founded in 1854, for many years dominated the traffic on the Sacramento and San Joaquin rivers. It was so profitable that it paid dividends of 300%. In the early 1870s it was sold to the Central Pacific Railroad (Southern Pacific) (Jerry MacMullen, *Paddle-Wheel Days in California* [Stanford, CA, 1944], pp. 20-23).

[40]Edward D. Baker was born in London in 1821. In Illinois he served in Congress, 1845-1846, resigning to serve in the army during the Mexican War. At the conclusion of the war, he was again elected to Congress. Baker came to California in 1852.

Also defending Cohen was Samuel M. Wilson. Born in Ohio in 1824, he married a daughter of John Scott, Missouri's first representative in Congress. Later, as a leading attorney in San Francisco, he represented such firms as Southern Pacific, Wells Fargo, and Bank of California.

9 when the jury brought in a verdict against Cohen and fined him $269,000. Cohen did not pay, and the judge imprisoned him once more for contempt. Only the State Supreme Court could act to release him, and two of its Justices were not available.[42] Not until he had spent weeks in jail did the Justices set him free. It took six years more of appeals and litigation for all the charges against Cohen to be acted upon. Finally they were dismissed. Hubert Howe Bancroft later wrote that "the press of San Francisco preferred to lay all blame upon and incriminate the most convenient person... Cohen was temporarily made the scapegoat for all."[43]

The 1856 decision against A.A. Cohen by no means ended the related litigation. Among the new suits was Edward Stanly's own claim in that same year against Woods and Haskell for $20,000. When the Superior Court set aside this suit early the next year, Stanly appealed to the Supreme Court of California, which upheld the decision of the Superior Court.[44]

However, in the spring of 1856 the Adams & Co. difficulties were overshadowed by new startling events. On May 14 the belligerent James King of William was shot by James P. Casey, who had the previous October become a member of the San Francisco Board of

[41] *Arguments of the Hon. Edward Stanly and T.W. Park, esq.; with the Charge of the Court at the trial of Alfred A. Cohen on charges of Embezzlement* (San Francisco, 1856).

[42] Justice David S. Terry was raised in Texas, where he became a Ranger. He served in the Mexican War and arrived in California in 1849; in 1855 he was elected to the Supreme Court of California. In a fracas with a member of the Vigilantes, Terry stabbed his opponent and was arrested by the Vigilance Committee. Another member of the Court, Justice S. Heydenfeldt, was traveling in Europe.

[43] Bancroft, *History of California*, vol 7, p. 178.

[44] *In the Supreme Court of the State of California, Alvin Adams vs. Isaiah C. Woods and Daniel H. Haskell in the matter of the petition of Edward Stanly, brief of Eugene Casserly, counsel for the Defendants* (San Francisco, n.d.).

North Point Warehouse at Sansome and Lombardy streets, built by Woods and rented to A.A. Cohen.

Courtesy: Society of California Pioneers.

Supervisors. The assault resulted in the formation of
the second Committee of Vigilance. After King's death
on May 20, the Committee hanged Casey, arrested
some, and banished still others. Historian Robert
Glass Cleland wrote that the law's failure in connection
with the Adams & Co. disaster "aroused the public's
discontent and served as one of the contributing
motives for the creation of the Vigilance Committee of
1856."[45]

As the legal battles continued, Naglee and his
attorney Stanly had a falling out. Naglee published a
pamphlet addressed to the creditors of Adams & Co.
critizing the actions of Palmer, Cook and Co. Stanly
defended the company, accusing Naglee of desiring "to
destroy" Palmer, Cook and Co.

Naglee continued his accusations, claiming Trenor
Park was $10,000 in debt to Adams & Co. as well as
"possessor of valuable property lately belonging to
Adams & Co." He stated that if Park "differs with
me... he condemns himself."[46] This was typical of the
bitter quarrels among all concerned during these trying
times.

In spite of the death of James King of William, the
Bulletin, under his brother, Thomas King, resumed its
attacks upon everyone connected with Adams & Co. It
claimed that Adams & Co.'s failure was the "greatest
fraud," that Woods called in an "unprincipled
lawyer... to assist him in carrying out his nefarious
designs." Casserly was referred to as "the prince of

[45]Robert Glass Cleland, *History of California, The American Period* (New York,
1923), p. 292.

[46]*Correspondence of Henry M. Naglee, Receiver to Palmer Cook and Company and
Edward Stanly, submitted by the former to the creditors of Adams and Co.* (San
Francisco, 1856).

cunning lawyers" to whom Woods had paid $50,000 of Mokelumne Hill canal stock. If this charge was true, Casserly received little of value as the company failed.[47]

Thomas King, like his brother, had his enemies. Assemblyman James Estell of Marin County, a former State Senator, attacked him in the State Assembly in 1857, referring to him as "Slippery Slim King," associated with a San Francisco brothel and as "crafty as a fox and slippery as an eel."[48]

Thomas King's continuous attacks on A.A. Cohen resulted in a fracas on February 12, 1857, when the combative Fred Cohen attacked King, beating him on the head with his cane. King responded by drawing his pistol and shooting Cohen. The wound was not serious. King was charged with assault with a deadly weapon, but all charges were dismissed three days later.

The widespread interest in all these events is reflected in songs and pamphlets of the period. Possibly the most popular song, "California Bank Robbers," was printed in 1858 in *Put's Golden Songster*.[49] The entertainer Mart Taylor, who also composed songs, traveled through the gold-rush towns with a company that included the little Lotta Crabtree, the darling of the miners. In 1856 he composed *The Gold Diggers' Song Book*, published in Marysville. While never as popular as *Put's*, it contained many of the argonauts' favorites. One song, sung to the tune of "Pop Goes the Weasel,"

---

[47]Jackson, *Twenty Years on the Pacific Slope*, p. 64.

[48]*Sacramento Daily Union*, Feb. 4, 1857. Thomas King was also the subject of some verses in Hugh McDermott's pamphlet published in San Francisco in 1857. In part he writes: "The Bulletin comes next in a more heinous sight... The editor (God help us) whose name is Thomas King... Of all groveling creatures he's the basest thing;... This loon with vile slander man's character doth cloud."

[49]John A. Stone, "California Bank Robbers," *Put's Golden Songster* (San Francisco, 1858), pp. 39-42.

recalls the stirring events in California of the mid-1850s. (See Appendix for the text of these songs.)

A popular pamphlet published in San Francisco in 1857 by Hugh F. McDermott, a printer by trade, was entitled *Poems: Epic, Comic and Satiric* and was dedicated to "Free lunchers and noodle-headed Scribblers." Included is "The Swindled Miner," about which he wrote: "This doggerel was written at the time of bank bursting in San Francisco." It too indicates the general feeling of that period in such lines as: "But kings or emperors ne'er played a part / Half so ruinous to the heart / As the scheming banker, whose hellish soul / Sells his warmest friend for gold."

Gradually the troubled affairs of Adams & Co. faded from public interest. As it turned out, most of the men who played leading roles in the company's failure went on to interesting and successful subsequent careers. Henry M. Naglee became a Civil War general and a leading citizen in San Jose, where he owned a large ranch. Trenor Park became wealthy through his acquisition of an interest in Fremont's Mariposa land grant. He returned to the East and became president of the Panama Railroad and a director of the Pacific Mail Steamship Company, then retired with his millions to his estate in Vermont.[50] Alfred A. Cohen built the San Francisco and Alameda Railroad, which he sold to the Central Pacific; after the Central Pacific became the Southern Pacific, he became a Southern Pacific attorney. Frederick Billings left California in the 1860s. He became president of the Northern Pacific

---

[50]Trenor Park sold his railroad interests for seven million dollars. His mansion in North Bennington, Vermont, as well as his second wife's home in San Rafael, California, are listed in the National Register of Historic Places. Kenneth M. Johnson characterized Park as a "pirate in a frock coat." *Journal of the West*, Jan. 1978.

Railroad, and Billings, Montana, is named for him.

Three of the men became United States Senators. Edward O. Baker was elected from Oregon. During the Civil War he was killed while leading his Union troops at the battle of Balls Bluff.[51] Eugene Casserly and Judge John Hager, who had presided over much of the litigation concerning Adams & Co., became United States Senators from California.

John T. Doyle became attorney for the Catholic Archdiocese of San Francisco and successfully developed the claims of the Church in the famous Pious Fund Case. His interest in California history led him to write scholarly articles and become the founding president of the California Historical Society. Alvin Adams became enormously wealthy during the Civil War. However, not all did so well. The fortunes of Daniel H. Haskell, who had drawn I.C. Woods into the affairs of the company, fell; he is said to have died in an almshouse.[52] In December 1858 Eugene Casserly wrote in a letter to John T. Doyle that "Haskell is here, broken down, going about here and at the Ranch (Pulgas) claiming as his own various articles. . . horses, carriages, furniture, etc."

The failure of Adams & Co. was so important an event in the chronicles of California that many of the leading state historians of the last century have written about it analytically. They all mention the fine buildings the company had built for protection from fire and thieves as well as to heighten its prestige. They have pointed out factors contributing to its failure, one

---

[51]Baker Street and Baker's Beach in San Francisco bear his name. Baker is buried in the Presidio.

[52]Noel M. Loomis, *Wells Fargo* (New York, 1968), p. 331.

being the State Constitution's ban on issuing paper currency.[53] The panic of 1855 directed the attention of Californians to the need of political reforms,[54] and it led to the formation in 1856 of the People's Party, which for many years governed San Francisco conservatively.

Historian John Hittell wrote, "the early banks were established and conducted by individuals with no training in the banking business." Further, he noted, "the newness of the country compelled the bankers to take great chances, fortunes being won and lost quickly."[55] He reported that "the assets of Adams & Co. became the subject of a general scramble by creditors and lawyers... most of the creditors got a trifle; some got payment three or five times over... most of the property was eaten up by litigation."[56]

Hubert Howe Bancroft agreed: "The poorer depositors, who were not able to fight against heavy odds, realized nothing, from first to last the public never understood how the disaster occurred or where the money went."[57]

Dwight Clarke, writing in the twentieth century, pointed out that nine years after Adams & Co.'s collapse "there was still a half million dollars owing to its luckless creditors."[58]

T.H. Hittell summed up the whole distressful affair

[53]Franklin Tuthill, *The History of California* (San Francisco, 1866), p. 402.

[54]Jackson, *Twenty Years on the Pacific Slope*, p. 61.

[55]John S. Hittell, *Commerce and Industries on the Pacific Coast* (San Francisco, 1882), pp. 126-27.

[56]John S. Hittell, *A History of the City of San Francisco* (San Francisco, 1878), pp. 232-33.

[57]Bancroft, *History of California*, vol. 7, pp. 178-79.

[58]Clarke, *William Tecumseh Sherman*, p. 117.

of Adams & Co.'s failure: "Everything from start to finish apparently had been done wrong or at least had turned bad."[59]

In the 1860s, with the advent of the Civil War, the failure of Adams & Co. became of little interest. In any case, there were no more funds left to fight over.

---

[59]Theodore H. Hittell, *History of California*, vol. 3 (San Francisco, 1898), p. 453.

OVERLAND TO THE PACIFIC.

THE SAN ANTONIO AND SAN DIEGO MAIL LINE, which has been in successful operation since July, 1857, are ticketing **PASSENGERS THROUGH TO SAN DIEGO**, and also to all intermediate stations.

Passengers and Express matter forwarded in **NEW COACHES**, drawn by six mules over the entire length of our line, excepting the Colorado desert of 100 miles, which we cross on mule back. Passengers guaranteed in their tickets to ride in coaches, excepting the 100 miles, as above stated.

Passengers ticketed to and from San Antonio, and

Fort Clark,	Fort Fillmore,
Fort Hudson,	La Mesilla,
Fort Lancaster,	Tucson, Arizona
Fort Davis,	Fort Yuman,
Fort Bliss,	San Diego.
El Paso,	

The Coaches of our line leave semi-monthly from each end, on the 9th and 24th of each month, at 6 o'clock A M.

An armed escort travels through the Indian country with each mail train for the protection of the mails and passengers.

Passengers are provided with provisions during the trip, except where the coach stops at public houses along the line, at which each passenger will pay for his own meal.

Each passenger is allowed thirty pounds of personal baggage, exclusive of blankets and arms

Passengers coming to San Antonio can take the line of mail steamers from New Orleans twice a week to Indianola; from the latter place there is a daily line of four-horse mail coaches direct to this place.

On the Pacific side, the California Steam Navigation Company are running a first-class steamer semi-monthly to and from San Francisco and San Diego.

Fare on this line as follows, including rations:

San Antonio to San Diego	$200
" " Tucson	150
" " El Paso	100

Intermediate stations 15c. per mile.

Extra baggage, when carried, 40c. ℔ ℔ to to El Paso; $1 ℔ ℔ to San Diego.

Passengers can obtain all necessary outfits in San Antonio.

For further information, and for the purchase of tickets, apply at the office of the Company, in this city, or address, I. C. WOODS, Superintendent of the line, care of American Coal Company, 50 Exchange Place, New York.

G. H. GIDDINGS, } Proprietors.
R. E. DOYLE, }

San Antonio, July 1, 1858.   27-tf

OVERLAND TO THE PACIFIC.

The San Antonio and San Diego Mail Line.

THIS LINE which has been in successful operation since July, 1857, is ticketing PASSENGERS through to San Diego, and also to all intermediate stations. Passengers and Express matter forwarded in NEW COACHES drawn by six mules over the entire length of our Line, excepting the Colorado Desert of 100 miles, which we cross on mule back. Passengers GUARANTEED in their tickets to ride in Coaches, excepting the 100 miles, above stated.

PASSENGERS TICKETED TO AND FROM SAN ANTONIO AND

Fort Clark,	Fort Bliss,	Tucson,
Fort Hudson,	El Paso,	Arizona,
Fort Lancaster,	Fort Fillmore,	Fort Yuma,
Fort Davis,	La Mesilla,	San Diego.

The Coaches of our Line leave semi-monthly from each end, on the 9th and 24th of each month, at 6 o'clock, A. M.

An armed escort travels through the Indian country with each mail train, for the protection of the mails and passengers.

Passengers are provided with provisions during the trip except where the Coach stops at Public Houses along the Line, at which each Passenger will pay for his own meal.

Each Passenger is allowed thirty pounds of personal baggage, exclusive of blankets and arms.

Passengers coming to San Antonio can take the line of mail steamers from New Orleans twice a week to Indianola; from the latter place there is a daily line of four horse mail coaches direct to this place.

On the Pacific side the California Steam Navigation Company are running a first class steamer, semi-monthly, to and from San Francisco and San Diego.

FARE ON THIS LINE AS FOLLOWS, INCLUDING RATIONS:

San Antonio to San Diego, $200   San Antonio to El Paso, $100
" " Tucson, 150   Intermediate stations 15c. per mile.

Extra baggage, when carried, 40 cents per pound to El Paso, and $1 per pound to San Diego.

Passengers can obtain all necessary outfits in San Antonio.

For further information, and for the purchase of tickets, apply at the office of the Company in this city, or address I. C. WOODS, Superintendent of the line, care of American Coal Company, 50 Exchange Place, New York.

G. H. GIDDINGS,
R. E. DOYLE,
Proprietors.

Posters of the San Diego and San Antonio Mail Line from the late 1850's.

III

Stage Coaches and Wagon Roads

When I. C. Woods left San Francisco so suddenly in August 1855, he went to Australia and then England, as he wrote A.A. Cohen he planned to do. As mentioned, he had left California with little gold. This is contrary to the opinion of many in California in the 1850s and some later writers as well, For example, Julian Dana wrote in 1936 in his biography of Ralston that "Woods decamped with a reputed two million dollars for Australia, a departure that effectively bankrupted Adams and Company."[1] Letters written at the time, however, indicate Woods was in need of funds shortly after he left California.

On June 2, 1856, the San Francisco newspapers reported he had arrived in England on the *Red Jacket*. On May 15 he had written from Brighton to Joseph Palmer of Palmer, Cook and Company stating he had met Judge Solomon Heydenfeldt of the California Supreme Court, who called Trenor Park a "scoundrel."[2] Woods told Palmer he would return to California if he was sure of a fair trail and asked Palmer

---

[1] Julian Dana, *The Man Who Built San Francisco* (New- York, 1936), p. 92.

[2] Solomon Heydenfeldt, a native of South Carolina, came to California in 1850. He was elected to the State Supreme Court in 1851 and served until 1857. He may have called Park a "scoundrel," but in 1857, after his retirement from the bench, he joined Park's law firm.

to consult with Eugene Casserly regarding this. He referred to Casserly as a "very firm friend and legal advisor."[3]

On September 5, 1856, the *Alta California* reported that another well-known San Franciscan, Sam Brannan, had met Woods in London. Brannan said that Woods would be soon returning to San Francisco, and the *Alta* added that Woods had since arrived in Canada. Early in the next year he was back in the eastern United States, however, initiating another venture.

Woods' long-time foe, the *San Francisco Bulletin*, described the endeavor in its issue of March 20, 1857. Woods had placed a notice in eastern papers stating that in an attempt to aid emigration, he was organizing an expedition "to California on the Western Frontier." The expedition would explore a new route to California and would consist of a party of about twenty-five men and eight or ten wagons. Its explorations would obtain new scientific knowledge on the route. Woods gave as references the names of three men: R.E. Doyle of San Francisco, James Birch of New York, and James Flint of Boston, the latter a member of the important San Francisco firm of Flint, Peabody. The *Bulletin* reprinted the announcement, then resorted to sarcasm:

> For cool unblushing imprudence it is the richest document we have read in a long time... There is no man living so calculated to give you correct information... he has visited England and Canada to keep out of the way of his accomplices and lawyer friends who are endeavoring to find the victims... the poor widow, helpless orphans, the hardy miner... who had so much confidence in his ability to safely

---

[3]Letter at the Huntington Library.

Eugene Casserly was Woods' attorney. A brother-in-law of R.E.
and John T. Doyle, he later became a U.S.
Senator from California.
Courtesy: California State Library

keep their money... You can expect this worthy I.C. Woods
to incur more expense for your sake.

Woods' plan did not materialize, but he continued
his interest in transportation. In April and May he
accompanied James B. Leach, who had been awarded
the contract to build a wagon road from El Paso to Fort
Yuma, on a buying tour on the East Coast to outfit the
expedition. Of this, more later.

A few weeks after, in June, Woods was named to a
position of importance by James Birch, who had
established the California Stage Company, one of the
largest and richest staging firms.[4] Birch appointed him
superintendent of the new San Antonio and San Diego
Stage Line, the first mail and passenger line to the
Pacific Coast. Birch and Woods had been friends in
California. When Woods was a principal in Adams &
Co., he had given Birch the bulk of Adams and Co.'s
shipments in the area served by Birch's California
Stage Company.[5]

James Birch, a native of Rhode Island who had come
to California in 1849, had developed successful stage
lines in the northern part of the state. When in 1854 the
California Stage Company was formed through a
merger of various stage companies, Birch became
president. Shortly after Adams & Co.'s failure, he
acquired for his company Adams' three-story brick
building in Sacramento. It had cost $85,000 to erect,
and Birch bought it at a Sheriff's sale for $28,000. This
historic structure still stands. However, late in 1855
Birch left California, and he was living in Massachu-

---

[4]William Banning and George Hugh Banning, *Six Horses* (New York, 1930), pp.
39-40.

[5]Hero E. Rensch, "Woods' Pioneer Shorter Mountain Trail," *Calif. Hist. Soc.
Quar.*, vol 36, (June 1957), p. 129.

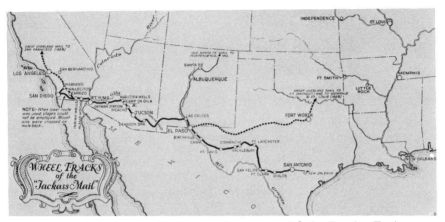

A map of the Jackass Mail route from an article in *Touring Topics*, November 1929.

A coach of the San Antonio-San Diego Stage Line crossing Arizona. From a painting by Marjorie Reed of Tombstone, Arizona, prepared for this publication.

setts when he appointed Woods superintendent of the new line.

California had hoped since 1850 for a safe, convenient passage by the transcontinental route to supplement that by sea. The demand for an overland route increased from year to year. In 1853 Congress appropriated funds for a study to determine the best route across the continent. However, the interests of the North and South clashed, delaying a solution. Finally, in 1857, Congress passed an act providing a subsidy for carrying the mail between the Atlantic and the Pacific, and bids were advertised on April 20.

The Postmaster General had the choice of selecting the contractor as well as the route. Aaron V. Brown, the Postmaster General, was born in Virginia in 1795, but had lived in Tennessee since 1815, serving that state as a congressman and governor. He chose a southern route. He was also a friend of Birch, and Birch had the experience and ability and was considered the logical choice to receive the $600,000 yearly grant. The *New York Times* on July 7, 1857, stated: "Mr. Birch is a gentleman of large capital and much experience and more competent, perhaps, than any other single man in the United States to execute this great mail contract." However, President Buchanan over-rode Brown's decision and rewarded an old friend, John Butterfield, with the prize. Birch was given the much less desirable contract for the San Antonio and San Diego Mail Line in the extreme southern part of the Union.

This route had been chosen because of the influence of the powerful Southern politicians in Washington. The *New York Times* claimed it was a route "least of all adapted to serve the public interest."[6] The northern

---

[6]*New York Times*, June 25, 1857.

California newspapers held similar opinions. The *Sacramento Union* stated the line "started in the middle and didn't go anywhere" and "terminates upon both sides at an unconvenient *[sic]* distance from the great commercial, financial and population centers."[7] Eugene Casserly wrote his brother-in-law, John T. Doyle, on October 19, 1857, expressing a similar opinion: "No doubt, the Southern route is the one by all odds... The trouble is when you are at either end San Diego or San Antonio you are not anywhere." (This opinion may, at the present time, be of interest to the residents of these large and important cities.)

The editor of *Hutchings' California Magazine* noted that everyone wished "to be better informed concerning this vast territory," but that "the question very naturally arises, Is this the most suitable method of obtaining it? We think not."[8] It was aptly described as "leading from no place through nothing to nowhere."

Birch received his contract for the line on June 23; the next day he appointed Woods superintendent. R.E. Doyle, Woods' brother-in-law, became the agent in San Diego, the western terminal. Casserly wrote John T. Doyle on July 12, 1857, that Emmet Doyle (R.E. Doyle) was

> ...going to San Diego to be Superintendent of this end of the mail route... I have talked with Emmet, he says he has no choice... his paper has dwindled away almost to nothing... Sarah [his wife, Woods' sister] insists on being with him; which I think right of her and the best thing for him if he is to live in San Diego.

In San Francisco, Henry van Valkenburg was appointed representative. He had been a trusted

---

[7]*Sacramento Union*, Oct. 1, 1857.

[8](James) *Hutchings' California Magazine*, vol. 2, no. 4 (Oct. 1857), p. 190.

employee of Adams & Co. and as such had received
much criticism from Woods' antagonists.

The line went into operation quickly. Mail was to be
carried by riders. Passengers were to be transported on
stage coaches. The first sack of mail started west by
horseback from San Antonio on July 9, 1857. Woods
had left for San Antonio a few days earlier with a
certificate of deposit of $20,000 to purchase horses,
mules, feed, etc. He traveled overland through
Chicago, Cairo, and New Orleans, thence by ship to
the Texas port of Indianola,[9] and arrived in San
Antonio July 11. There, greatly aided by G.H.
Giddings, a skilled stage-line operator,[10] he was able to
make his purchases. Finally, on July 24, the first coach
left with the mail. On July 31 Woods and a party of men
followed with supplies consisting of saddles, bridles,
blankets, arms, and rations, as well as mules.

The trials of Woods' trip from San Antonio to San
Diego were many. There were encounters almost
immediately with hostile Indians, resulting in loss of
mules and property, and deaths. When he got to El
Paso, he was able to obtain more animals. On
September 8 he reached San Diego. There the arrival of
the first transcontinental mail was a signal for a
celebration. The *San Diego Herald* reported "a hundred
anvil salute, and the firing of pistols and rifles."[11]

Casserly wrote John T. Doyle on September 18,

---

[9]Indianola, Texas, now vanished, was the port in Matagorda Bay. Floods in 1875
and 1886 destroyed the city. The business of the town was transferred to Port
Lavaca.

[10]George H. Giddings was a native of Pennsylvania. In 1853 he organized the
San Antonio-Santa Fe Stage Line via El Paso. In 1857 he became agent of the San
Antonio and San Diego Mail. At the outbreak of the Civil War he joined the
Confederates, lost his wealth, and died in Mexico in 1902, according to R.P. and
M.B. Conkling in *The Butterfield Overland Mail* (Glendale, CA, 1947).

[11]Richard P. Pourade, *The Silver Dons* (San Diego, 1963), pp. 220-21.

1857, that Mrs. I.C. Woods "went to San Diego to meet her husband who persists in his determination to return to California."

Woods in his 1858 report to the Postmaster General claimed that R.E. Doyle, as agent for the western division of the line, "had advanced the money needed to commence service on the Pacific end of the line." Before he left San Diego, Woods placed advertisements in numerous California newspapers advising the public that the line was ready to ticket passengers from San Francisco to New Orleans via San Diego, Fort Yuma, Tucson, Mesilla, Ft. Fillmore, El Paso, and San Antonio. A notice in the *San Francisco Herald* gave the office of the stage line as Kearny Street "opposite the Plaza." The "experienced Stager," Charles McLaughlin, was listed as the San Francisco agent.[12]

Woods and Doyle reached Fort Yuma on November 5, 1857, and there received the "melancholy news" of the death of the 29-year-old James Birch. On September 12, en route to the East Coast, he had perished when the ship *Central America* sank near Cape Hatteras. The anger over the loss of the *Central America*, as well as the condition of other ships, is reflected in a song of the period from *Put's Golden Songster* (1858):

Loss of the "Central America"
(Air—"Carry me back to old Virginny")

The "Central America," painted so fine,
    Went down like a thousand of brick,
And all the old tubs that are now on the line
    Will follow her, two at a lick.

---

[12]Charles McLaughlin's career is recorded in Charles Outland's *Stagecoaching on El Camino Real* (Glendale, CA, 1973).

'Twould be very fine were the owners aboard,
  And sink where they never would rise;
'Twould any amount of amusement afford,
  And cancel a million lies.

....

These murdering villains will ne'er be forgot,
  As long as America stands;
Their bones should be left in the ocean to rot,
  And their souls be at Satan's commands.

On December 4, 1857, Casserly reported these events to J.T. Doyle:

Emmet has come up here from San Diego by the last steamer, so far as I can judge with the intention of making further contracts in reference to the Mail Route. I remonstrated with him of assuming any further personal liability or investing any more of his means... of his own money he has put in and spent $4,000... He has also put in some $11,000 belonging to old Mrs. Woods [I.C. Woods' mother] with her consent... Emmet says without doubt the contract will pay *net* $90,000 to $100,000 a year, which may be, but in other hands than those of I.C. Woods who has proved himself all his life visionary, reckless and unsuccessful to the last degree... It is reported the Butterfield party who have the weekly contract were purchasing the Birch contract. It is so obviously their right interest to buy it, that I think the event extremely possible... while affairs are in this critical position at New York, Woods is away of course, a part of his usual luck. He must come to this end, when he was not wanted, for no earthly reason I can discover except to see his wife and to alarm his friends. Consequently upon hearing of Birch's death he set off on his return at once; Emmet says he could not have reached New York before December 10, of course too late... It is, I suppose, in the fates that he is to lose this contract and with it his only "living chance" of redeeming himself in this world ... No doubt great fortunes have been made out of mail contracts; but I think it must have been by those who had capital and an acquaintance with the business. There is another side of the picture of the kind of life led by contractors whose associations are necessarily almost entirely with the wildest and rudest men in the world. Yet Emmet seems almost carried away by the idea of trail contracts and he went off yesterday to San Diego, carrying Sarah with him, though I urged him to leave her at least until he knew that he was to remain permanantly at San Diego.

Doyle returned to San Diego while Woods continued on to San Antonio. There further disturbing news awaited him. On October 26, Birch's widow had revoked his authority and had placed her stepfather, Otis Kelton, in charge. Giddings, the San Antonio superintendent, soon objected to Kelton's interference in the management and threatened to withdraw his support.

Woods, on his own, returned to the East Coast and with other friends of the late Birch was able to "smooth out the ruffles.[13] The letters of Casserly to John T. Doyle in the early part of 1858 indicate this was not done with ease. On March 21, 1858, Casserly wrote:

> Emmet's affairs in the Mail Route do not clear up... yet I could not help showing Emmet how all the present trouble was, and future difficulties would be, the result of I.C.W.'s infernal trick of putting entire faith in nobody and always that cursed self-conceit of his which makes him the best judge of how much he will disclose and how much withhold, even in dealing with his counselors and friends, who have risked their all for him.

Casserly continued that Emmet had placed "$15,000 in the mail line against $20,000 put in by Birch."

However, On April 4, 1858, Casserly was elated when he wrote of the settlement with Mrs. Birch and Otis Kelton.

[13]Banning and Banning, *Six Horses*, p. 113.

The news of the great change of affairs in the matter of the
Overland Mail Route received here by last mail was
gratifying as it was unexpected... I could not see that the
triumph was so complete as it seems. Pretty clearly from
Woods' letter, the P.O. Department was desirous to transfer
the contract to Giddings & Co. but could not do it under their
rules, until default was made in carrying the mail by the
Birch interest. Then Woods advised Emmet to have a default
take place which was probably not difficult as Emmet at this
end and Giddings at the other end had virtual control of the
whole stock... If this matter is now fixed right at
Washington, I should not be [at] all surprised, from what I
hear of the probable failure of the great Butterfield contract,
if the San Antonio Route was raised to a weekly mail at the
same rate as the Butterfield, which of course would make the
eternal fortunes of the whole concern.

It appears that Woods also gained the support of the
Postmaster General. Under a new arrangement he was
reinstated as superintendent, with headquarters at 50
Exchange Place, New York, and Birch's contract was
transferred to Giddings and R.E. Doyle, who became
"proprietors" of the line.[14] Woods' 1858 report
indicates he was in the Southwest during the winter of
1857-1858.

However, from its very start the San Antonio and San
Diego Mail Line had financial difficulties. Woods
stated in his report that he had expected to meet Birch
in San Diego and receive additional cash. Since Birch
had died and he had not received it, he had sold "drafts
to cancel large amounts due to creditors." Because
Birch's estate was in probate, his funds were not
available for use by the stage line. Additional capital
became difficult to obtain, for the United States was
experiencing a commercial crisis following the

[14]*Ibid.*, p. 114.

national "panic of 1857." The line struggled on with financial troubles until the advent of the better financed Butterfield Overland Mail in September 1858 led it to a minor but stable role in transcontinental mail service.

Advertisements in the *San Antonio Ledger* on October 9, 1858, stated: "Passengers and Express matter forwarded in new coaches, drawn by six mules over the entire length of our line, excepting the Colorado desert of 100 miles, which we cross on mule back." They claimed they left San Antonio for San Diego "semi-monthly" and that an "armed escort travels through the Indian country with each mail train." To get to San Antonio, "passengers can take the line of mail steamers from New Orleans" and "on the Pacific side, the California Steam Navigation Company are running a first-class steamer semi-monthly to and from San Francisco and San Diego." For further information, readers were directed to "apply at the office of the Company, in this city [San Antonio], or address I.C. Woods, Superintendent of the line, care of American Coal Company, 50 Exchange Place, New York." In 1859 a similar advertisement appeared in the *Texas Almanac*. The fortitude of the passengers is indicated by the description at that time of a "Tucson bed" which the traveler made by lying on his stomach and covering himself with his back.

Two interesting items relating to the San Antonio and San Diego Line bear comment. The enterprise has often been referred to as the "Jackass Mail," a term first used contemptuously in the 1850s by the northern California newspapers displeased with the route. It was repeated during the line's centennial celebration in 1957, but, as has been written, "a mule is not a jackass."[15] Horses failed, and the mule was the animal that saved the day.[16] Another sidelight is the suggestion in the *San Francisco Herald* of November 13, 1857, that the mule on the overland mail be replaced by the camel!

It appears that I.C. Woods was considering returning to California. John T. Doyle wrote to the prominent San Franciscan George Gordon regarding this plan. Casserly, after reading Doyle's letter to Gordon, wrote on July 19, 1858, as follows:

> . . . the effort to manufacture public opinion in his favour, it is the judgement of all of us, might produce the direct contrary result. Finally I am of the opinion (Gordon not concurring) that the time will not have come, even by next January, when he can appear in San Francisco with safety to himself against criminal proceedings. The individuals are still alive and too many are still smarting under the bitter sauce of having been robbed by him of their all to permit those indictments to slumber. In case of a trial we could, I presume, change the venue to some other county, if we could find one where his victims have not poisoned the common mind.
>
> His overland telygraph *(sic)* is of course a grand project and ought to conciliate the public toward him, but in any case, I do not at all see how his presence in S.F. is to help it or him.

This may refer to a new project of Woods'; if so it was not fulfilled. Several years later Edward Creighton, in 1861, completed the first transcontinental telegraph line for the Western Pacific.

Historians of this century have praised Woods' management of the San Antonio and San Diego line. Such was not the case, however, in San Francisco in the late 1850s. His reputation remained tainted by the Adams & Co. failure, and he was often referred to in the

---

[15]Rensch, "Woods' Pioneer Shorter Mountain Trail," p. 132.
[16]Edwin Corle, *The Gila, River of the Southwest* (New York, 1951), p. 217.

newspapers as the "notorious Woods." On March 4, 1858, the *Alta California* mentioned the arrival of "I.C. Woods, esq." in New Orleans on his way to Washington. Two days later the *San Francisco Bulletin* published a letter from a citizen objecting to the use of "esq." after Woods' name. The writer suggested "a journal might as well try to dress in decency a woman lost to shame" or call Henry Meiggs "an enterprising citizen." The *Bulletin* added a comment in its usual manner, referring to Woods as the "notorious swindler...who planned and successfully robbed the people of this state of millions of dollars."

On July 23, 1858, even the less censorious *Alta* stated Woods' line was "of no benefit except to put money into the purses of the contractors." And on October 11, 1858, the same paper, while praising the new Butterfield route, referred to the "notorious I.C. Woods" as the "ruling spirit" of the San Antonio and San Diego Line on the extreme southern route.

As mentioned, the "Great Overland Mail" contract had been lost by Birch when President Buchanan awarded the plum to John Butterfield. Birch had been given only seventeen days to get his line into operation, but Butterfield had been given a full year to prepare. On September 16, 1858, the famous Butterfield Transcontinental Stage Line started its coaches across the southern route to California. The *San Francisco Bulletin* of October 11, 1858, claiming the "young giant of the Pacific is free," recorded the arrival of the first coach in San Francisco, which was celebrated in a meeting in the Musical Hall.

There Woods' line was not entirely ignored. Frederick P. Tracy, San Francisco's City Attorney, praised the new line but gave credit to the San Antonio and San Diego Mail Line as well:

> For months past we have been receiving mail from San Antonio, Texas, by way of El Paso, a route identical with this very road for a considerable distance. I doubt not the increased speed on this part of the road which has been spoken of is in good measure owing to the experience of that pioneer mail line. I would give due credit to those engaged in the San Antonio and Fort Yuma route.[17]

A few months later, on March 8, 1859, Postmaster General Brown died. Judge Joseph Holt of Kentucky, the new Postmaster General, decided the mail lines to the Pacific Coast were too costly. For example, he found that the annual compensation of the San Antonio and San Diego Line was $196,448, the receipts, $601; the Butterfield Line received $600,000, its receipts, $27,229; while the Pacific Mail Company received $738,750, with receipts of $299,472. To reduce costs the San Antonio and San Diego Line's service was reduced from weekly to semi-monthly and its compensation lowered to $120,000 annually. This same year, 1859, the San Antonio and San Diego Line received approval from the *Texas Almanac:* "It is certainly a remarkable fact that not a single failure has yet taken place under this important mail contract. If any proof could be sufficient to satisfy the world of the superior advantages of this route for a railroad to the Pacific, it should be such proof as this."

A major factor that had increased the difficulties of

---

[17]*Sacramento Union*, Oct. 12, 1858. Frederick Palmer Tracy, a native of Connecticut, had been a Methodist preacher and editor before he came to California in 1849. He practiced law and became City Attorney of San Francisco, 1857-1859. He died in New York while stumping the state for Lincoln. His daughter became the wife of John Swett.

the stage line was the costly depredations of the Indians. Again and again station hands were killed, coaches demolished, and hay burnt. Often the raids left only charred walls of the wooden stations. Frequently the marauders stole or destroyed the stock, including the valuable mules. One marvels at Giddings' and Woods' perseverance in continuing to run the stage coaches on their perilous journey.

Shortly after the Butterfield Line started its operations, the San Antonio and San Diego Line's central section between El Paso and Fort Yuma was said to have been abandoned. However, the *San Antonio Ledger and Texan* carried an advertisement on July 2, 1860, and again on August 18, 1860, indicating that the San Antonio and San Diego Mail Line was still operating from San Antonio through El Paso and Fort Yuma to San Diego, and stating, "As a winter route this possesses many advantages over all others." These advertisements were signed: "I.C. Woods, Superintendent."

That the Mail Line was still attempting to obtain new federal subsidies is indicated in Casserly's letter of June 4, 1860:

> With respect to the Overland-Butterfield matters of which you write so fully... I have for some time back thought a good deal and I am sorry to say after many efforts I can not get up the interest which for Emmet's sake I would like to feel... While I.C.W. is "Captain, mate and all hands" in that concern, I can not excite myself... I regard that man with disgust as a most uncommon mixture of impudence, conceit, rascality... Am convinced that while his influence on Emmet lasts, he will keep him poor, and unless it is removed, he will ruin him... I like Emmet very much and Sarah also and further would do anything for him... But for I.C.W. I can have no feelings but sovereign contempt and

dislike, aggravated by the continual fear of his any day doing something to cast disgrace on us all, in addition to what he has already brought on us.

   Having said this I add that I will write Latham [U.S. Senator Milton Latham] as strongly as I can, in deference to your evident wishes... I fear the $300,000 per annum, should they get it, would go where the $190,000 per annum has already gone under I.C.W.'s evil star... Theresa [Doyle's sister] agrees with me in all this... I have confidence in her judgement.

Although on December 1, 1860, the Postmaster General stated the whole line was "entirely useless,"[18] it continued in operation until the Civil War. It lasted until August 1861, a few months after the Butterfield line closed down.

   I.C. Woods' *Report to the Hon. A.V. Brown, Postmaster General, on the Opening and Present Condition of the United States Overland Mail Route between San Antonio, Texas, and San Diego, California*, 1858, remains a remarkable and important document in the history of the opening of the West. In it Woods wrote vividly of the difficulties encountered and the wonders seen on the first journey along this mail line. He gave a meticulous description of the country the line traversed, with a table of distances between all the watering places along the 1,475 miles.[19]

   The significance of the San Antonio and San Diego Mail Line was that it was the first line to make possible trans-continental transportation, moving both people and mail. As Ralph Moody wrote in his *Stagecoach West*, "the operation stands as a landmark in American

---

[18]*San Diego Hist. Quar.*, vol. 3, no. 2 (1957).

[19]Woods' 1858 *Report* is listed in Wagner-Camp, *The Plains and Rockies*, indicating its importance. Also, R.P. and M.B. Conkling, in their three-volume history of *The Butterfield Overland Mail*, call it an "enlightening report on the southern route" (vol. 1, p. 94).

history."[20] According to another twentieth century history, William and George H. Banning's *Six Horses*, it was due to I.C. Woods "that the wheels continued to turn."[21]

During the years 1857-1858, while he was active in the mail line, Woods was also involved in another transportation enterprise. This gained him no glory, however, and led to his indictment by the United States government.

For many years Californians had been appealing to Congress for improved roads across the nation, which they hoped some day would be the routes of railroads. In April of 1856, 60,000 residents signed a memorial to Congress urging such a road. Finally, in 1857, Congress appropriated funds to improve the existing central overland road, to build a southern overland road, and to lay down roads into New Mexico and the Minnesota frontier.

Jacob Thompson, a longtime Congressman from Mississippi, was selected by President Buchanan to be Secretary of the Interior, the department given responsibility for the project. This was in contrast to most federal road-building in the West, which had been under the auspices of the War Department. However, during this same period, 1857-1858, the Army did survey a road along the thirty-fifth parallel through the Territory of New Mexico (which included the present Arizona). This was north of the Interior Department's road from El Paso to Ft. Yuma. In 1853-1854 Amiel W. Whipple, of the United States Topographical Engineers, had surveyed this route along the thirty-fifth parallel. Chosen to head this new

[20]Ralph Moody, *Stagecoach West* (n.p., 1967), p. 88.

[21]Banning and Banning, *Six Horses*, p. 113.

wagon-road survey was Edward Fitzgerald Beale. He left San Antonio on June 25, 1857, for the West with his wagon train, which included camels![22]

The contract for the southern route from El Paso to Fort Yuma, known as the Pacific Wagon Road, was awarded to James B. Leach, a Californian, on April 22, 1857.[23] Leach had had experience in building and improving roads in the Salt Lake region in 1855. Leach chose as chief engineer a man of known ability, N. Henry Hutton.

As his own assistant Leach selected a friend, a former Californian, whose name was given as "D. Churchill Woods." It was perhaps an error, repeated in the early correspondence of the El Paso and Fort Yuma wagon road, although it may have been a conscious attempt to avoid the criticism that mention of the name I.C. Woods frequently aroused. Curiously, Woods' signature on the letter in the wagon road correspondence appears to read "D. Churchill."[24] However, by 1859 he was referred to in the reports as "I. Churchill Woods," and this was the name given in his later indictment. However, the San Francisco newspapers reporting Woods' difficulties continued to identify him as the "notorious I.C. Woods of the Adams Express."

As already mentioned, in 1857 Woods had

---

[22]Edward Fitzgrald Beale (1822-1893) during the Mexican War performed heroic deeds at the Battle of San Pasqual. In 1848 he brought to Washington some of the first gold from California, and he became owner of the famous Tejon Ranch. Beale will always be remembered for his part in the importing and use of camels in the Southwest; he believed the experiment was successful, but they were not accepted and finally disappeared. See Carl Briggs and C.F. Trudell, *Quarterdeck and Saddlehorn: The Story of Edward F. Beale* (Glendale, CA, 1983).

[23]W. Turrentine Jackson, *Wagon Roads West* (Berkeley, CA, 1952), pp. 218-232.

[24]Correspondence on microfilm at San Bruno, CA, Office of the National Archives.

accompanied Leach on a tour of the East coast markets to outfit the expedition. Memphis, Tennessee, was selected as the departure point of the wagon train carrying the supplies, and on June 27 it left for El Paso.[25] It slowly crossed Arkansas, Indian Territory (the present Oklahoma), and continued through Texas to El Paso. By October 22, 1857, the advance party had reached El Paso, but the ox-drawn wagons did not arrive until June 25, 1858, almost a year after their departure from Memphis.

Communication with Washington was slow and difficult; nevertheless, work on the wagon road proceeded as planned. However, the Secretary of the Interior became alarmed by the increasing expenditures, the delay in presenting verified vouchers, and rumors of misconduct. Finally he ordered an investigation into the possibility of fraud.

Amongst the charges that were made were two that directly reflected upon Woods' double association with the San Antonio and San Diego Line and the wagon road. It was alleged that some of the road builders' property had been used to transport mail by the San Antonio and San Diego Line,[26] and that mule teams bought for $900 were sold in San Diego to "one R.E. Doyle with the San Antonio and San Diego Mail" for a fraction of their cost.[27] The investigator, W.B. Sayles, who looked into these charges claimed that he found discrepancies in the vouchers, the amounts submitted to the government being more than was actually paid to the providers. In May 1858 Leach was relieved of duty

[25]Jackson, *Wagon Roads West*, p. 222.

[26]Letter from Sayles to Thompson, June 17, 1858. Welcome B. Sayles had been appointed a "special agent" by Secretary Thompson.

[27]Letter from Sayles to Thompson, Feb. 4, 1858.

and his chief engineer, Hutton, appointed super-intendent.[28]

Woods was indicted by the federal grand jury and appeared before the United States Commissioner in New York City. The *Alta* of May 8, 1858, reported "the notorious Woods" of the Adams Express Co. had been examined and that there was "seemingly no end to the frauds against the public" because there were false vouchers amounting to $200,000. Other California newspapers reported the case in a similar fashion. However, the Commissioner exonerated Woods, concluding that he made "no profit in the transactions" and that the difficulties were the result of "mistaken views of the law."

Casserly wrote Doyle on December 19, 1858, referring to this latest development in Woods' affairs.

> A man like him covered with suspicion is worse than insane to expose himself to accusations of even technical offenses and then what becomes of his position and influence at Washington when it was so vital to himself. He must be an utter fool or worse, probably both... Sometimes I wish the name of Woods was blotted out of the world... Emmet has relapsed into Woods' frenzy and has it worse than ever... But I hope the return to the East of Mrs. I.C. Woods with the little Woodses will tend to keep him there.

On March 4, 1859, Casserly wrote:

> I feel much about the U.S. prosecution against Woods. It would be such a public disgrace reflexing more or less upon all of us were he to be indicted and tried and still worse of such a charge. Emmet's connection with the family [his wife being Woods' sister] make such things a deep and painful concern to all of us. I hope he will get off and learn a little prudence and decency for the future.

---

[28]Letter from Thompson to Leach, May 4, 1859.

Casserly also wrote Doyle on May 4, 1859, after the Commissioner exonerated Woods:

You have done very well in Woods' case in obtaining from Commissioner Belts so successful a decision... The Alta this morning had a most savage leader, containing many details I hear were obtained from a discarded employee of the Wagon Road. It also suggested that the private malice of Kelton and others have had much to do with this prosecution. I shall make some influence to weaken the blow here as far as possible, though in truth I don't feel inclined to trouble myself a great deal for such a combination of conceit, folly, ingratitude, selfishness and total absence of moral principle as this person so manifestly is. Any other man could have been cleared against this charge very readily — there being no crime in clerical error... I wish the Lord would take him whenever he is ready to go which I fear however will give him a longer lease of life than Methuselah! Really I do think after having got him through this last affair, you are not called on to trouble yourself anymore. What is worse he seems to have thrown a glamour over Emmet who I think would follow him to the very gates of the Penitentiary.

Casserly wrote in a similar manner on November 20, 1859: "He [Emmet] is utterly controlled by I.C.W. like Mephistopheles in Faust."

Woods' troubles seemed never to be over, however. A couple of months after his clearance, he was arrested in New York,[29] charged with "forgery and fraud," and escorted by a United States Marshal to Texas. There he was to be tried in a case recorded as the "United States vs. I. Churchill Woods." Albert Campbell, General Superintendent of all the Pacific wagon roads, was scheduled to testify against Woods, but neither he nor any other witness appeared, and again Woods escaped punishment. The case was dismissed.

[29]Woods was arrested November 17, 1858.

Woods' work on the wagon road received some praise, however, from M.A. McKinnon of Mississippi, the disbursing agent of the expedition. He wrote, "Captain D.C. Woods *[sic]* persevered with all possible vigor and energy against numerous obstacles which he met," and continued with additional approving remarks about Woods' activities.[30]

Charges were brought against Leach, but they too were later dropped. Campbell wrote on March 7, 1861, to the Secretary of the Interior that witnesses against Leach would be difficult to find, as the present location of some were unknown. He also stated that the Texas witnesses would not be available (apparently because Texas had joined the Confederacy in February 1861), so there was no way to prosecute.[31] The Civil War was starting, leaving little interest in the case.

Superintendents of other wagon roads also faced charges of misconduct.[32] According to W. Turrentine Jackson, the Department of the Interior was partly responsible for problems, for it had no tested organization to supervise these road projects, no efficient bookkeeping system, and no former experience in wagon-road building. And, as the historian noted, "complexity also encouraged dishonesty."[33]

Leach presented an excellent, but probably overly optimistic, report to Superintendent Albert Campbell on January 29, 1859; it was addressed to the Secretary of the Interior.[34] In this twenty-page report, largely written and signed by Hutton, the engineer, Leach was quite enthusiastic about the route between El Paso and

---

[30]Letter at National Archives, San Bruno, CA.
[31]Campbell's letter, National Archives, San Bruno, CA.
[32]Jackson, *Wagon Roads West*, pp. 186-190; 322.
[33]*Ibid.*, p. 322.

Fort Yuma. He claimed there was wood available sufficient for cooking and a supply of water for the travelers and their animals. He stated the road "shows its superiority over all other roads to the Pacific" and praised the "mildness of the weather" along the route. The most valuable section is the detailed description of the road by Hutton, who also praised it as "the shortest route... the favored route for speed and safety." Further, he claimed, new variants of the route had been located that had better supplies of water and that shortened the number of miles, thus saving several days of traveling time to the Pacific Coast.

There was a difference of opinion regarding the superiority of this road. The *San Diego Herald* on July 5, 1858, stated the new road was opened and "in first rate for traveling," with an "abundance of water and grass along the entire line." It continued that "Colonel Leach's" road "is shorter by upwards of a hundred miles" than the old road and "large and substantial tanks have been erected all along the line."

However, a contrary view was expressed on March 3, 1859, in Arizona's first newspaper, *The Weekly Arizonian.* Under the title "Leech's *[sic]* Wagon Road," it stated: "Before Congress grants further appropriations for 'wagon roads' we venture the suggestion that some official investigation be instituted as to the expenditures made and the work done by the late expedition." The article continued:

> The amount of labor performed was very trifling... as to the

---

[34]*Report of Pacific Wagon Roads*, 38th Cong., 2nd Sess., Senate Doc. 108, Feb. 23, 1859.

Jacob Thompson resigned from the Cabinet, January 7, 1861, and returned to Mississippi; he became War Governor and aide to General Pierre G.T. Beauregard of the Confederate Army.

road along the Gila, we doubt very much if it has ever been
traveled by a wagon since the expedition left, and the first
tracks... are growing up to grass... The water tanks... are
the meanest ever laid out... These celebrated 'tanks' excite
ridicule... [we] confess a thorough disgust for the small
amount of labor and the immense quantity of bloviation
[verbose and windy oration].

Eugene Casserly's letters disclose his dislike for his
relative by marriage, I.C. Woods. He appears to have
had concern about how Woods' actions would reflect
on the honor of his family. Also Casserly had anxiety
regarding the effect on his political career, which
culminated in 1867 in his election to the U.S. Senate.[35]

Thus, as usual, the activities of I.C. Woods were
marked by controversy. The latter half of the 1850s did
not bring him wealth or great credit, but he did make a
contribution to history as a pioneer in opening the
Southwest. Years later, the route of the San Antonio-
San Diego Line between Fort Yuma and San Antonio
became the path of the Southern Pacific Railroad,
while Beale's wagon road became the route of the Santa
Fe Railroad.

---

[35]The excerpts from Eugene Casserly's letters to John T. Doyle in New York are
from the collection of Mr. and Mrs. Merlin W. Porter, Jr., of San Francisco.

IV

Civil War Years with Fremont

Woods' association with transcontinental transportation plans and with controversy did not cease. In the spring of 1860 the *New York Times* published a letter entitled "Memorial of Californians in New York," which was reprinted in San Francisco newspapers on May 23. It was signed by Peter Donahue, a founder of the first iron works and later the first gas works in San Francisco, Theodore Payne, a wealthy San Francisco real estate auctioneer, and George Gordon, founder of the first sugar refinery in California, who probably wrote it. The "Memorial" urged support of a bill introduced by United States Senator John Hale of New Hampshire which would create an Overland Mail Route and would, of course, spell the death of the Butterfield line. The San Francisco businessmen claimed that if the California representatives in Congress supported the bill, it would pass.

The letter implied that the powerful Senator William M. Gwin of California had been working against the bill in behalf of the Pacific Mail Company, which would be injured by improved overland transportation. It was an accusation not new in California. A wrathful Gwin replied in a letter published in the *San Francisco Bulletin* on June 9, maintaining that Gordon had been led into error "by designing men, the most adroit of whom is I.C.

Woods," that their aim "was not to promote the public interest but to put money into their pockets," and that the desire of I.C. Woods is "to break the Butterfield contract." Gordon did know Woods, having dealt with him in his San Francisco South Park real estate development. In addition, John T. Doyle, Woods' friend and relative, was living in New York at that time and was George Gordon's attorney and confidant. Doyle wrote Woods that he, too, was working for Hale's bill and that Senator Milton Latham, of California, appeared to be favorable toward it.[1]

Senator Hale's bill did not pass, and the *Alta* of July 24 claimed Senator Gwin was a factor in the defeat. Historian Robert G. Cleland, writing about transportation in California before the transcontinental railroad, claimed the Pacific Mail, with a $700,000 yearly government subsidy, was a "powerful, well-organized opposition" to all transcontinental mail routes.[2]

However, events were moving closer to the Civil War, which would permanently close not only what remained of the San Antonio and San Diego Mail Line but the Butterfield Overland Mail as well. Lincoln's election in 1860 was followed early in 1861 by a meeting of delegates from seven Southern states and the formation of a provisional government. In Woods' obituary in the *San Francisco Bulletin* it was claimed that Woods was sent to South Carolina by the War Department on a secret mission to report on the conditions of affairs in that state. But Woods himself, testifying before the Joint Committee of Congress in

[1] J.T. Doyle's letter, Bancroft Library, Univ. of Calif., Berkeley.
[2] Robert C. Cleland, "Transportation in California before the Railroad," *Hist. Soc. of Southern Calif.*, vol. 11, part 1 (1948), p. 63.

1862, merely stated he was "in Charlestown on my way to Texas [apparently to straighten his financial affairs in that state] when Fort Sumter was bombarded."[3]

The Civil War began. Woods went north to Baltimore, where, according to his obituary, he was present when the Baltimore mob stoned and fired upon the Sixth Massachusetts troops passing through on their way to defend Washington. Southerners tore up the tracks of the Baltimore and Ohio Railroad, and Woods was reported to have aided in the railroad's reopening. However, Woods stated only that he "proceeded to Baltimore,"[4] where he aided the Union forces.

In Maryland, Woods was associated with the important Blair family that strongly supported the Union. Woods may have known the Blairs through James Blair, who had lived in San Francisco in the earlier gold-rush period. They had many associates in common.[5] It was through the Blairs that he came to serve with General John Charles Fremont. The elder member of the family, Francis Preston Blair, James Blair's father, had lived many years on his Maryland plantation, "Silver Springs." He was a leader of the Lincoln forces, which were decidedly in the minority in that predominately secessionist state. Woods

[3]*Conduct of the War, Report of the Joint Committee*, Washington, D.C., 1861-1863, p. 212.

[4]*Ibid.*

[5]Personal letter from Joseph W. Smith, son of Professor William E. Smith of Miami University, authority on the Blair family. James Blair owned property in San Francisco and in the present Ventura County with his attorney, Eugene Casserly. He was also a claimant to the Mexican land grant Rancho Salsipuedes in the Pajaro Valley. After James Blair's death in 1852, the family conveyed to Eugene Casserly on January 14, 1853, a half interest in the ranch. Montgomery Blair remained a part owner. Also, James Blair had John T. Doyle prepare a suit against W.H. Aspinwall of the Pacific Mail.

recalled that it was the Blairs who recommended him to
General Fremont when he was appointed Commander
of the Department of the West, because of his
transportation experience. When Woods testified
before the Joint Committee of Congress, he was asked,
"Who recommended you to General Fremont?" He
answered, "Montgomery Blair. I had been doing
business for his department for three years."[6] This
recalled Woods' association with the transcontinental
mail line and its dealings with the United States Post
Office Department, of which Montgomery Blair, as
Postmaster General, was now in charge.

On September 9, 1861, Woods officially entered the
United States Army as a volunteer with the rank of
captain and was assigned to the Commissary
Department.[7] General Fremont gave him responsibility for transportation in Missouri, and apparently he
carried out his duties well, for Fremont soon promoted
him to major, then colonel.

Woods' duties must have been varied. *Harper's
Weekly* carried articles on Fremont and his staff that
autumn. A full-page illustration in the October 12,
1861, issue shows General Fremont and his staff, all
mounted, "Inaugurating Camp Benton, Missouri"; in
the caption listing the names and ranks of the staff,
"Colonel J. [sic] C. Woods" is described as an "Aide-
de-camp."[8] Elsewhere he was called Fremont's
"personal secretary" and "adjutant."[9] He himself
simply stated he was placed "in charge of transportation."[10]

[6]*Conduct of the War*, p. 212.

[7]Francis B. Heitman, *Historical Register and Dictionary of the United States Army*,
vol. 1 (Washington, D.C., 1903), p. 1058.

[8]*Harper's Weekly*, October 12, 1861, p. 644; also September 14, 1861, p. 582.

[9]Noel Loomis, *Wells Fargo* (New York, 1968), p. 331.

[10]*Conduct of the War*, p. 331.

The Blair Family
Left to right: Francis P. (Frank) Blair, Jr.; Francis Preston
Blair, Sr.; and Montgomery Blair.
From *The Francis Preston Blair Family in Politics*, by William E. Smith
(N.Y., 1933).

By reporting to General Fremont, I.C. Woods had allied himself with one of the most controversial figures in American history, and he found himself embroiled in a dispute between a Missouri member of the Blair family and the general. The Blairs had long been Fremont's supporters. Abraham Lincoln called him the Blair's "pet and protege." They helped Fremont receive the Republicans' nomination for president in 1856. Defeated by James Buchanan, he retired to his Mariposa Estate in California and later to Black Point in San Francisco, but at the outbreak of the Civil War the powerful Blairs persuaded President Lincoln to place him in charge of the Department of the West, with headquarters in St. Louis, Missouri. Another member of the family, Francis (Frank) Blair, Jr., was an important citizen of Missouri.

When Fremont arrived in St. Louis on July 25, 1861, he found conditions chaotic, money scarce, and asses, horses, and mules in short supply. While the German people of St. Louis, a minority, greeted Fremont enthusiastically, most of the important residents were sympathetic to the Confederacy. On August 10 the Missouri Union forces received a painful blow when General Nathaniel Lyon was killed and his troops defeated at Wilson Creek.[11] Frank Blair, an intimate friend of Lyon's, blamed Fremont for not heeding Lyon's call for reinforcements. Actually, Fremont, who was Lyon's superior, had ordered him to retreat, but he had failed to do so.

Blair, who was a Congressman from St. Louis and leader of its Union supporters, was not one to

---

[11]General Lyon is remembered in California for establishing the San Diego barracks in 1851 and for leading his troops against the Indians at "Bloody Island," in Lake County, in 1850. Lyon Street in San Francisco is named for him, as are Lyons [sic] Valley and Lyons Peak in San Diego County.

MAJOR-GENERAL FREMONT, U.S.A. AND STAFF INAUGURATING CAMP BENTON, AT ST. LOUIS, MISSOURI, BEFORE STARTING FOR LEXINGTON.—FROM A PHOTOGRAPH.—[SEE PAGE 604.]

Major-General John C. Fremont and staff inaugurating Camp Benton at St. Louis, Missouri. This engraving is from the issue of *Harper's Weekly*, October 12, 1861, which lists the names of Fremont's staff, including "Colonel J. [*sic*] C. Woods, Aide-de-Camp."

antagonize. As Catherine Phillips in her biography of the General's wife, Jessie Benton Fremont, stated, "When the Blairs go into a fight, they go in for a funeral."[12] Blair was outspoken, claiming the Californians in Fremont's retinue "had settled down" in St Louis "like obscene birds of prey" and that they "enjoyed special confidence and favor."[13] On September 19 he wrote of "the distribution of contracts to worthless and corrupt hang-ons from California,"[14] men who in St. Louis were called "foreigners."[15]

On August 31 Fremont issued his famous controversial proclamation, which called for emancipating all the slaves belonging to Missourians who cooperated with the Confederates. Washington received this action with less than enthusiasm, to state it mildly. The timing was poor, as Lincoln was still devoted to the task of trying to keep the border states, such as Missouri and Kentucky, from entering the Confederacy.

The conflict with Frank Blair reached a climax when Fremont arrested him for "insidious and dishonorable efforts to bring my authority into contempt." The Blairs reacted at once. Francis Blair, Senior, had been an important figure in American politics since the time of Andrew Jackson. One son was a member of Lincoln's cabinet. Thus it is not surprising that early in November President Lincoln removed Fremont from his position as Commander of the Department of the West. The "One Hundred Days" of his ascendancy were over.

---

[12]Catherine Coffin Phillips, *Jessie Benton Fremont, A Woman Who Made History* (San Francisco, 1935), p. 246.

[13]*Conduct of the War*, pp. 176-78.

[14]William Ernest Smith, *The Francis Preston Blair Family in Politics*, vol. 2 (New York, 1933), p. 80.

[15]*Ibid.*, p. 69.

Fremont was charged with neglect of duty, disobedience to orders, gross extravagance, mismanagement, misappropriation of public funds, and despotic conduct. His friends urged an investigation, and a Congressional committee was formed.

John T. Doyle advised Woods in a letter of November 30, 1861, "one thing is clear to me, you are not to identify yourself with the defense of the General. If you do you will be crushed in his fall. Ask for active service somewhere you can be of use... Write Sherman... the General is a used up man."[16]

Woods, however, did not heed Doyle's advice. He testified at length before the Joint Committee of both Houses of Congress investigating the charges against Fremont. It appears from his testimony that Woods had been a close associate of General Fremont's. He told how "the day the General was superceded, I think it was Saturday, the 2nd of November, I rode out with the General to the outer pickets." Also, the following Monday after General Fremont had made his farewell address and was riding out of Springfield, Woods recalled, "I rode out with the General then, riding just in rear of him."[17] When asked about the charge that Fremont had been too exclusive and refused to see visitors who wished interviews, Woods answered that Fremont "was not exclusive enough"; he also added that "Blair was free to interview Fremont at all times."

Woods defended himself as well as the General. He told the Committee that he "had no interest with contracts" and further that he had "sacrificed as much

---

[16]J.T. Doyle's letter, Bancroft Library. The expression "used up man" was in common use in the 1850s. A popular gold rush song was entitled "The Used Up Man" (see *Hangtown Ballads* [Georgetown, CA, 1948]).

[17]*Conduct of the War*, p. 206.

as any man ever did sacrifice, for I had large interests in
Texas before the War, I sacrificed the whole of it."

When Frank Blair was asked by the Committee
about I.C. Woods, he replied, "I never heard of his
(Woods') having any contracts." He continued:

> I was present when my brother recommended him to
> Fremont verbally ... He told Fremont that Woods had
> proved very serviceable to him in the post office department
> as sort of a spy, or rather as an agent for organizing a spy
> corps; and by his energy in getting the mails through
> Baltimore at the time of the interruption; and also in putting
> the custom-house and post office officers into their places
> from which they had been excluded by fear of the mob; he
> had showed courage and tact in this service. He thought he
> would be serviceable to Fremont in the same capacity...
> Fremont said he knew Woods well, in California, and
> coincided in my brother's judgement of his [Woods'] activity
> and sagacity... I will say here that in all the testimony I have
> seen and heard in regards to Woods, although I...have
> heard since that his name in California was not very good, I
> have never heard of any thing that has been brought home to
> him of a criminal character in regards to contracts.

Frank Blair added, however, that Fremont's aides
from California were "Californians of the worst
possible reputation in California." They included
Joseph Palmer of the former San Francisco bank of
Palmer, Cook and Company, a close friend of Woods;
Leonidas Haskell, like Palmer a San Francisco
neighbor of Fremont's; Elias Lyman Beard of Mission
San Jose;[18] and the former San Francisco auctioneer,
A.A. Selover.[19] The last two had been associated with
Fremont's fight for the Mariposa grant.

---

[18]Elias Lyman Beard owned hundreds of acres at Mission San Jose in the 1850s.
M.W. Woods' *History of Alameda County* (1883) has praise for Beard's actions in St.
Louis in 1861.

The *Chicago Tribune,* quoted by the *Alta California* in San Francisco, denounced the "California Gang," attributing to it all the "corruption around Fremont." It claimed too that Woods as "Director of Transportation" in Missouri and "private secretary" of Fremont had failed to provide proper transportation for the troops of Illinois, Iowa, and Indiana, and his "remissions and neglect have been the cause of much misery." The *Alta* concluded that "Fremont has California associates to thank for all his trouble" and that "he should have dismissed Woods and Palmer."[20]

While Woods denied all charges in "cards" in the newspapers, the impression remained just as it had after the fall of Adams & Co. that there had been shady dealings. Woods defended himself, relating his difficulty in obtaining wagons, horses, mules, and especially harnesses. He explained that

> ... the greatest difficulty encountered in providing transportation was to procure the requisite number of harnesses. The shops in St. Louis were engaged in making cavalry equipment and artillery harness as well as team harness, but their capacity is comparatively limited. The facilities in Chicago and Cincinnati were also limited, and besides both cities had large orders to fill for infantry equipment for their State troops.

Woods also presented to the Committee a large number of written orders relating to this problem that he had sent as "Colonel and Director of Transportation."[21]

Shortly after Fremont was relieved of duty on

[19]Abia Selover, a Mexican War veteran, served as an alderman in San Francisco in 1850. He became a successful and well-known San Francisco auctioneer, of the firm of Selover and Sinton. Selover did not return to San Francisco after the Civil War. He died in the East in 1898.
[20]*Alta California,* Dec. 3, 1861.
[21]*Conduct of the War,* pp. 215-16.

November 9, 1861, Woods resigned from the Army. The *San Francisco Bulletin*, still on the trail of the "notorious I.C. Woods," indicated on February 3, 1862, that his resignation had been refused and that he was being detained in Missouri, as charges might be leveled against him. This was untrue; Woods at that time was in Washington, D.C., testifying before Congress.

The *Bulletin* also published a letter from "Colonel Woods" to General Lorenzo Thomas, Adjutant-General of the Army, replying to certain accusations regarding the purchase of water kegs. Woods declared these charges were malicious, as the questioned water kegs had not been bought but had been given free to the Army. While the *Bulletin* published this denial by Woods, it again referred to him as "notorious I.C. Woods." Other California newspapers at that time used similar terms of opprobrium.

The Congressional Committee, after investigating, found the Fremont administration in Missouri to be characterized by "earnestness, ability and most unquestionable loyalty,"[22] but Fremont's Army career was drawing to an end. He had been sent to West Virginia and ordered to cross the mountains, a wilderness with no roads, into Tennessee to aid the Union Army in that region. With a poorly equipped army, it was an impossible task. Unsuccessful, he resigned from the Army. In October 1863, he also lost his San Francisco home when the United States Army was ordered by the Secretary of War to take possession of Black Point, on which his residence and those of Joseph Palmer and Leonidas Haskell were located.

---

[22]Quoted in Cardinal Goodwin, *John Charles Fremont* (Stanford Univ., 1930), p. 231.

None of them ever received compensation, although for a hundred years petitions and court actions were continued by their heirs.[23]

A final California note might be of interest, since it indicates that Frank Blair's accusation against the "California Gang" may have been based on his displeasure at not having his St. Louis friends receive contracts rather than on any lofty ideals. Fighting for ownership of the valuable New Idria quicksilver mine in what is now San Benito County, William McGarrahan distributed stock to members of Congress, including "the Hon. Francis Blair, M.C., from Missouri," who received 3,200 shares.[24] But in the end they proved worthless; the Supreme Court rejected the claim on the basis of fraud.[25]

The *New York Illustrated News* on June 18, 1864, stated that "His [Fremont's] views on the Slavery question and military policy were, however, so far in advance of the Administration's that it contrived to have charges of personal corruption trumped up by the Blairs, none of which have ever been substantiated, and made them the excuse for relieving him of his command of the Western Department in the midst of the most important and successful operations."

I.C. Woods' actions under Fremont, while criticized in the newspapers, were found to be correct and honest by the investigators. Once more he had begun a promising career only to have it end in disappointment.

[23]Lois Rather, *Jessie Fremont at Black Point* (Oakland, 1974), pp. 87-90; and *Letter from the Secretary of War*, 43 Cong., 2nd Sess., Ex. Doc. 26, 1875.

[24]*History of the McGarrahan Claim as written by himself* (pamphlet), in Bancroft Library, pp. 146-87.

Also, *Panoche Grande*, Argument of Titian J. Coffey, esq., against the McGarrahan Claim (Washington, D.C., n.d.), p. 16.

[25]Sources cited above and Francis Parker, "McGarrahan's 'Panoche Grande Claim,'" *Pacific Hist. Rev.* (Sept. 1936), pp. 212-21.

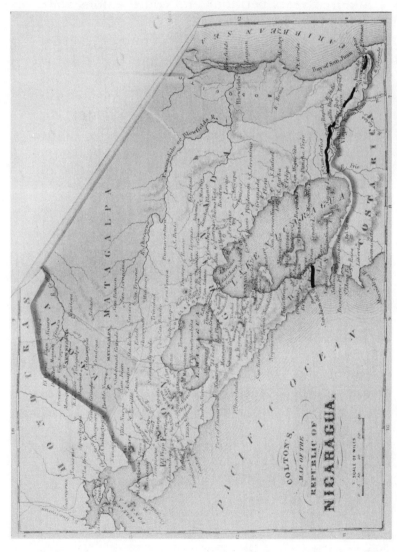

A nineteenth century map of Nicaragua, showing the passenger route of the
Central America Transit Company.

V

In Nicaragua

I.C. Woods' next endeaver involved another transportation scheme. In November 1861, shortly after Fremont's St. Louis debacle, Mrs. Woods arrived from California with her three children to join her husband in Washington. During this trying time for Woods, John T. Doyle wrote him several letters showing his interest in his welfare. In April 1862 Doyle wrote that his good friend Holladay would aid Woods. A month later he informed Woods he was returning to California with Holladay by the overland route. This appears to be Ben Holladay, soon to be the new "Stage Coach King." However, Holladay apparently did not associate Woods with his Overland Stage Line.

Robert Emmett Doyle, writing from his Menlo Park estate in 1862, reported to his brother, John T., that Woods' "Missouri Expedition is broken up" and "by this time [he] must admit to himself his turning soldier was a grave error." Doyle also mentioned that "Old Mrs. Woods" (I.C.'s mother) would soon join their household in Menlo Park.[1]

Woods wrote on April 16, 1861, to S.L.M. Barlow of the Overland Stage Line[2] that he had been asked to

---

[1]Letters at the Bancroft Library.

[2]S.L.M. Barlow was an associate of Ben Holladay. When Holladay left the Overland Stage Line in 1866, Barlow was in charge for a short time before Wells Fargo took over. Later, Barlow ran stage lines in Colorado.

command a regiment in New Mexico, "with an invading army into Texas," but that he had refused this offer.[3] Apparently he had had enough military adventures. According to the obituary of Woods in the *San Francisco Bulletin*, he then became associated with Francis Morris, president of the Central American Transit Line, and went in its behalf to Nicaragua. There he "started a line of transportation" across the narrow neck of land from the Atlantic to the Pacific and had "surveys made for a railroad."

The route across Nicaragua was many hundreds of miles shorter than the Panama route. This was a fact recognized by George Gordon in 1849, when he led his "Gordon California Association" across Nicaragua, the first organized party to use this passage to the California gold fields.[4] Later, Cornelius Vanderbilt developed this route, his ships successfully competing with the Panama route. Unfortunately, the passage was virtually closed in 1855 because of turmoil created in Nicaragua by the filibuster, William Walker.[5] It remained in disorder until Walker's execution in Honduras in 1860.

In 1861, however, the Central American Transit Company obtained a charter from the Nicaraguan government, and in 1863, after the company had financial troubles, Francis Morris was named the new president. Morris endeavored to have the road repaired, and he purchased vessels for connecting the Nicaragua isthmus with both Atlantic and Pacific

---

[3]Letter at the Huntington Library.

[4]Albert Shumate, *The California of George Gordon* (Glendale, CA, 1976), pp. 67-88, 94.

[5]John T. Doyle had known Walker in San Francisco and wrote that Walker's book, *The War in Nicaragua*, was written in his (Doyle's) "parlour" in New York City.

ports. Advertisements of the "Opposition Line" (opposing the dominant Pacific Mail line) named the S.S. *Golden Rule* on the Atlantic side and the S.S. *Moses Taylor* on the Pacific. The announcements claimed this route to be the "shortest and quickest" to California. In San Francisco, I.W. Raymond, a well-known Californian, became agent.

Morris sent Woods to Nicaragua in 1864. On his arrival at Managua, the capital of Nicaragua, Woods informed the United States Minister there, Andrew B. Dickinson, of the plans of the Transit Company to open the route for transportation. Dickinson notified the Nicaraguan officials that Woods was the "Special commissioner and chief representative of the Company."[6] Dickinson's letters always referred to Woods as "Col. Woods," recalling his Army career, short as it was. Dickinson, in his official capacity, endeavored to aid the Transit Company in its difficult negotiations with the Nicaraguan government. He also kept his superior, Secretary of State William H. Seward, well informed of the onerous trials of the company.

Woods put the route in repair. It was macadamized,[7] and fifty Concord coaches were procured, ready to convey passengers. Also, river steamers were placed in commission for the part of the route along the San Juan River and across Lake Nicaragua. In August 1864 the line was reopened.[8]

However, again Woods found himself working for a company that had financial troubles. Morris failed to cure them, and neither he nor his successor, William

---

[6]Certification of I.C. Woods, 1864, National Archives Branch, San Bruno, CA; M No. 219, Roll 14, Vol. 8.

[7]As early as 1855 the Nicaragua Steamship Line had advertised "a macadamized road" in Nicaragua (*San Francisco Bulletin*, Nov. 2, 1855).

[8]David I. Folkman, *The Nicaragua Route* (Salt Lake City, 1972), pp. 113-14.

H. Webb, nor anyone else could solve the company's principal difficulites. They were caused by the constant demands of the often-changing governments of Nicaragua and the gradual filling with silt of the main Atlantic port, San Juan del Norte. The loss of their steamer *Golden Rule* on May 30, 1865, did not help. Then, because of its financial weakness, the Transit Company was unable to build the railroad from Lake Nicaragua to the Pacific Ocean that the charter called for. Its stock fell from $102 per share in 1864 to zero in 1867. In an attempt to save the firm, President Webb advertised in the newspapers that the company was in good condition and able to transfer passengers without difficulty from the East to California. Nevertheless, the Central American Transit Company failed in 1868.[9] Dickinson had advised the United States government to aid the company, but no aid was given. All interest was focused on the building of the transcontinental railroad, a feat accomplished in 1869, dooming all other passenger routes to California.

Once more I.C. Woods was left adrift. He may have left the company after president Morris's departure from the firm and before its failure, for in February 1866 he was in London. George Gordon wrote from England to his attorney, John T. Doyle, that he had seen I.C. Woods, who had "conveyed the lots to me and that is all that is wanted."[10] This may relate to lots 46 and 47 in block 104, near Third Street in Gordon's South Park development in San Francisco. They had been conveyed to Adams & Co. on September 30, 1854.

---

[9]*Ibid.*, p. 122. Webb sought William T. Ralston's aid, but was refused. Later, Ralston did aid Webb in developing a mail service from San Francisco to Honolulu and Australia.

[10]Letter of George Gordon, California Room, State Library, Sacramento, CA.

Gordon had a promissory note to that firm. When Woods' property was sold at auction by the Sheriff in 1855, claimants of Adams & Co. attempted to obtain this property but failed.[11] Woods, in January 1857, consigned these lots back to Gordon, and Gordon retained possession of them; the London transaction apparently completed the consignment.[12] The Doyles also had trouble in clearing the title to the former Woods estate in the present Menlo Park-Atherton area.[13]

Woods was in New York in the latter part of 1866 and early 1867, according to letters from John T. Doyle. In February 1867 Woods wrote Doyle from 52 New Street, New York, asking him to investigate certain claims of his in El Paso. Two months later, on April 16, Woods wrote Sam Ward from "Elizabeth" (Elizabethtown ?), New York, asking his help in a "delicate matter." He explained that in 1854 he had had A.A. Cohen purchase a 50-vara lot (137 1/2 by 137 1/2) at the corner of Post and Stockton streets in San Francisco, for which he had reimbursed Cohen. The ownership of this lot was to have been transferred to Mrs. Woods, but had not been. Woods told of the "brotherly and financial intimacy which subsisted between Alfred A. Cohen and myself up to the catastrophe of Feb. 22, 1855," and added that "our relations continue to be amicable as ever and I want no shade to come between us — though separation of our respective abodes of course has interrupted any other than a friendly community."

---

[11]Chief claimants were Joseph and William Palmer of the banking house of Palmer, Cook and Company, and Martin J. Burke, who served as Chief of Police in San Francisco, 1858-1865, and was a founder of the long-time real estate firm of Madison and Burke.

[12]Deeds regarding this property in author's collection.

Woods explained in a roundabout way his financial situation, how he had worked "to support my family and educate my boys properly," that he had "given my best efforts to public measures placing remuneration as a secondary consideration," and "how small and precarious is the present measure of my worldly means." He wrote of "the brave woman who has stood by me unfalteringly through good and through evil report," and reminded Ward that Cohen had "prospered in wealth and reputation" and that he could be expected to "do what is fair and honorable to Mrs. Woods." He concluded by asking Sam Ward to see Cohen about the matter.[14] Woods' friendship with Sam Ward had been a long and, as will be shown later, a helpful one.

While Woods' Nicaraguan venture did not meet with success, he had performed efficiently, repairing the road, having fifty Concord coaches ready to convey passengers, and putting two lake and six river steamers in commission.[15]

[13]J.T. Doyle letters, 1863 and 1866, Gleeson Library, Univ. of San Francisco.

[14]Letter from I.C. Woods to Sam Ward, Apr. 16, 1867, at the Henry E. Huntington Library, San Marino, CA.

[15]Folkman, *The Nicaragua Route*, p. 113.

VI

Back to California

I.C. Woods himself returned to California probably in 1868. Once more he was involved in a project that appeard to promise success. He is listed in the *San Francisco Directory of 1869* as living at 11 Kearny Street, and he registered to vote on August 30, 1869. The Woods family moved within the city several times during the next few years, which were apparently years of relative prosperity. In 1870-1872 they lived on Second Street near South Park. Later, their home was on Third Street, opposite South Park. In 1873 Woods became a member of the California Academy of Sciences.

He had not been in San Francisco long when his mother died, at the age of 66. Her death occurred on May 8, 1869, at the home of her daughter and son-in-law, R.E. Doyle, in Menlo Park. Her funeral was held at the residence of F.H. Woods on Pine Street, San Francisco, which indicates that Francis Woods' dislike for I.C. Woods did not prevent him from being friendly with other members of the family.

Woods had returned to California because he had been named manager of the Pacific Wood Preserving Company, which had obtained the so-called Robbins patent for a new process for preserving wood.[1] The company had been incorporated on March 29, 1869, capitalized for $500,000, with 5,000 shares valued at

$100 a share. The trustees included R.E. Doyle, which may have accounted for Woods' appointment as manager. Other trustees were well-known Californians.[2] One was John D. Fry, William C. Ralston's father-in-law.[3] He had been placed on other boards by Ralston during this period when Ralston was developing numerous new industries in San Francisco.[4]

It was the claim of the Pacific Wood Preserving Company that their method would protect wood from the teredo, the "shipworm" notorious for destroying ship timber, wood piles immersed in sea water, and other wood in harbors.

The 1869 report of the State Harbor Commissioners of California stated: "The preservation of submerged wood has for many years exercised the minds of savans *(sic)*... the Robbins Patent has been adopted by our State Harbor Commissioners as the best preventative against the teredo... superior to anything yet discovered for the preservation of wood." It noted that

---

[1]The Pacific Wood Preserving Company had purchased the patents of the "Robbins Process" from the National Patent Wood Preserving Company of New York, of which Luis H. Robbins was secretary. The Certificate of Incorporation, dated March 31, 1869, is in the California State Archives, Sacramento.

[2]Other trustees included Andrew J. Moulder, Alvinza Haywood, and H.B. Tichenor. Andrew J. Moulder had been Superintendent of Public Instruction for the State of California, 1857-1862. In 1868 he became the first secretary of the Board of Regents of the University of California. John T. Doyle was also a member of the Board of Regents, as was his brother-in-law, Eugene Casserly, a few years later.

Alvinza Haywood made a fortune in the Comstock. In 1869 he was a firm friend of William Ralston. His estate in San Mateo was well known.

H.B. Tichenor, a lumber dealer, also controlled the San Francisco Dry Dock, a project started in 1866 with Ralston's aid, as well as Tichenor's Shipyard. In 1873 he owned the controlling stock in the Los Angeles and San Pedro Railroad when it was transferred to the Southern Pacific.

[3]Actually Colonel John D. Fry was Elizabeth Ralston's uncle. After her family's death, Col. Fry assumed her care, and she took his name.

[4]David Lavender, *Nothing Seemed Impossible, William C. Ralston and Early San Francisco* (Palo Alto, CA, 1975), pp. 14-15.

An advertisement from the catalog of the Mechanics Institute
Fair of 1872.

"fifty thousand feet of surface plank had been preserved from decay and attacks of the ship worm under the Robbins Process by the Pacific Wood Preserving Company." The process was described as "infusing into the pores of the wood (after removing the albumen) the hydrocarbon oils from coal tar or petroleum."[5]

The City of San Francisco also gave official approval, enhancing Woods' firm's prospects. The City Board of Supervisors, on October 25, 1870, passed an ordinance designating this method for use in preserving the boards in the city's sidewalks and streets, which at that time were partially planked.[6]

In an advertisement dated December 1871 but published in the catalogue of the Mechanics' Institute Fair of 1872, I.C. Woods noted that his company had been awarded a gold medal by the Mechanics' Institute in 1871 and a special medal by the State Agricultural Society the same year. He further stated that wood preserved by his process had been adopted for use in bridges, wharfs, street planking, sidewalks, and cellar floors. He pointed out that "such wood pavements would be cheaper for the taxpayers and property owners... than cobblestone pavements as a free gift," for "it can be demonstrated that the money value of the horses, horse shoes, and vehicles destroyed by the use of cobble pavements is enormous." In 1872, reflecting the firm's expanded interest, the name of the company was changed to "Pacific Wood Preserving Company and California Paving Company."

The firm's office in 1869 was located at 407

---

[5]The Report of the Harbor Commissioners was printed in the *San Francisco City Directory of 1869* and again in that of 1870, p. 15.

[6]This ordinance was printed in the *San Francisco Municipal Reports, 1871-72.*

California Street. In 1871 it moved to 388 Montgomery Street. The "works" were at Berry Street near Fourth, beyond the city's main business section.

At first the company appeared to prosper. On November 5, 1871, however, the Berry Street workshop was destroyed by fire. The *Alta California*, on November 6, reported the fire was due to the "carelessness of a Chinaman" who held hot pitch near a flame. There was no insurance on this building, which had cost $65,000. Also lost was a large order from the Central Pacific Railroad. This was the company's second fire in eighteen months, for its first works, located on King Street, had also been destroyed. These disasters undoubtedly were factors in the subsequent failure of the venture, probably in 1875.

In 1876 the *San Francisco Directory* no longer listed the Pacific Wood Preserving Company and California Paving Company. A Sacramento newspaper later reported, "The process did not answer so well as was expected and comparative failure was the result."[7]

Marsdon Manson, a later City Engineer of San Francisco, reported in 1885 that the piles "along the wharf on East Street [Embarcadero] between Mission and Howard," which were treated by the Robbins Process in 1870, had to be rebuilt in 1878-79, "showing a failure of the process." The process failed also with another wharf on East Street treated in 1871. His conclusion was that the Robbins Process of creosote saturation was "flimsy."[8]

Another factor leading to the company's failure may have been that, regardless of Woods' arguments, the wooden streets of San Francisco were gradually being

---

[7]*Sacramento Daily Record-Union*, Feb. 18, 1880.
[8]*Transactions of the Technical Society of the Pacific Coast*, July 1885.

paved with cobblestone. In fact, the Superintendent of Public Streets, on June 30, 1875, reported: "All wood pavement should be removed... and replaced with stone blocks."[9]

The closing of the factory coincided with the sudden death of William C. Ralston and the collapse of many of his enterprises. If Ralston had indeed helped finance this company, as he may have, it well could have suffered the fate of many of his other projects.

It is of interest that Daniel H. Haskell's name, often missing from the San Francisco Directories after the failure of Adams & Co. in 1855, appeared in the directory of 1871 as a bookkeeper for the Fashion Stables on Sutter Street. The next year, 1872, he was listed as a bookkeeper at Woods' Pacific Wood Preserving Company, remaining at this position until the closing of the firm three years later.

The failure of this business after such an auspicious beginning must have been another severe blow to Woods. The *San Jose Pioneer*, recalling the event, stated, "For the first time the ill success appears to have dispirited even one of Mr. Woods' hopeful disposition."[10]

[9]*San Francisco Municipal Reports, 1874-75*, p. 134.
[10]*San Jose Pioneer*, Feb. 18, 1880.

VII

The Last Years

Daunted perhaps, but still active, I.C. Woods next became associated with the well-established trading firm of Balfour, Guthrie and Company. This affiliate of the Liverpool, England, house of Balfour, Williamson and Company had entered San Francisco in 1869. In its first years in California it dealt mostly in wheat, the great crop in the state at the time. It remained an important company in San Francisco for over a century,[1] but Woods' affiliation with it was brief.

The year of 1875 will always be remembered by San Franciscans as the year the Bank of California closed and its president, William C. Ralston, died. San Francisco's business was shaken, and by 1877 the depression was widespread in the state. In 1876 Balfour, Guthrie, like many others, had experienced a loss, and the firm reacted by a "reduction of activities."[2] By 1877 Woods was unemployed again.

This depression also affected Woods' brother-in-law, R.E. Doyle. Since 1867 he had been associated with I. Friedlander, the "Grain King," who failed after Ralston's death. In an attempt to aid Friedlander, R.E. Doyle had pledged land and money, most of which was

---

[1] In the 1920s Balfour, Guthrie's headquarters were located in the Balfour Building, now known as the Stanley Dollar Building.

[2] Wallis Hunt, *Heirs of a Great Adventure, the History of Balfour Williamson and Co. Ltd.*, vol. 1 (London, 1951), p. 98.

lost, some to the firm of Balfour, Guthrie and
Company, who were one of Friedlander's main
creditors.[3]

Doyle had moved to Nob Hill after he sold most of
his Menlo Park estate with I.C. Woods' old country
home to Kate Johnson on May 17, 1875. On July 29,
1891, she gave it to the Catholic church for St. Patrick's
Seminary. Woods' prefabricated frame house, which
had been brought around the Horn, burned in July
1909.[4]

Woods' next undertaking would be his last. It grew
out of an old friendship which recalls the fantastic
speculations in the Western mines during the early
1870s. This was a time when great fortunes were made
and lost by daring men — men like William C. Ralston,
William Sharon, E.J. (Lucky) Baldwin, George
Hearst, and somewhat later the new "Comstock
Kings," Fair, Flood, O'Brien, and Mackay. All
amassed great fortunes.

In this mining stock gambling, none was more bold
or more successful than James Robert Keene, in whose
employ Woods now found himself through the good
offices of their mutual friend, Sam Ward. Keene, born
in England in 1838, came to the United States when
young. He had drifted westward, and in California, ill
and friendless, he had been befriended by Sam Ward.
He rose quickly. By 1875 he had, through his stock
speculations, made a fortune estimated at between four
and five million dollars. Moving to New York, he
continued his daring stock manipulations on Wall
Street and increased his fortune to twelve million by
1880.[5]

[3] Friedlander Papers, Calif. Hist. Soc. Library, San Francisco.
[4] *Redwood City Democrat*, July 1909.

James R. Keene was a California and Wall Street speculator and
was owner of a great stock farm in Kentucky which produced
some of America's famous race horses.

As already indicated, there was a warm friendship between Ward and Woods. Ward always remembered Woods' kindness to him in California in the 1850s. Writing in 1861, he recalled a meeting with Woods in the Mariposa gold fields. "I little dreamed, when the light and active little man [Woods] shook hands with me and bespoke our 'bridal stateroom' for the night, that the future had in store for us vicissitudes and associations to which I recur with unalloyed satisfaction."[6]

Ward suggested to Keene that he employ Woods as manager of his ranch at Mission San Jose.[7] Keene had purchased the 1,500-acre ranch from Elias L. Beard, a pioneer of the area who had been one of Fremont's so-called "California Gang" in St. Louis.[8]

Woods also continued to be listed in the *San Francisco Directories* from 1877 through 1880 as residing in the city at various addresses on California Street on Nob Hill. It may be that his family remained in San Francisco, or that he stayed at the ranch only part of the time.

Woods has been reported as being ill the last few years of his life. However, he entered into his new career with his usual energy. The Mission San Jose area had early become a locality noted for its vineyards and winemaking.[9]

---

[5]Keene met with financial reverses in 1884, but regained his fortune. His Kentucky stock farm produced some of America's outstanding race horses. He died on January 3, 1913. Keeneland, Kentucky, commemorates his name.

[6]Carvel Collins, ed., *Sam Ward in the Gold Rush* (Stanford, CA, 1949), p. 164.

[7]*Ibid.*, p. 165. The *Alameda County Directory* listed Woods as "agt." at the "ranch of J.R. Keene." Also, for the friendship between Ward and Keene, see Lately Thomas, *Sam Ward, King of the Lobby* (Boston, 1965), pp. 398-400.

[8]Beard's residence was later owned by the Gallegos family and is now the Mother House of the Sisters of the Holy Family.

Again, with characteristic zeal, Woods was embarking upon a new enterprise. He was instrumental in developing a vineyard and winery on Keene's ranch. Wines from Keene's property were exhibited in 1878 by Woods at the Thirteenth Industrial Exhibition of the Mechanics' Institute. They were shown under the name of "Mission San Jose vineyard, James R. Keene, owner." Woods wrote that the Mission grape, was the predominant variety grown in the Keene vineyard.

Also in the catalogue of the Exhibition, the Committee on Wine answered some of Woods' questions. He inquired about the desirability of mixing Mission grapes with foreign grapes and naming the wine after the foreign variety, and of mixing several foreign grapes and naming the wine after the most prominent variety. The Committee stated that the mixing of different types of grapes was done in Europe and was permissible, but to sell the wine under the name of the most renowned grape was fraud. They further stated that there was no fraud if the wine was sold under the name of the vineyard, district, or town. The use of the name "claret" was allowable, but not "French claret."

This time, however, death ended yet another of Woods' enterprises. Early in 1880 Woods' health was failing, and he went to live with his brother, Dr.

---

[9]Clemont Colombet had been winning prizes for his wines since 1856. He briefly owned property in nearby Warm Springs, which he sold to A.A. Cohen. Cohen sold this land to Leland Stanford in 1869. Under the management of his brother, Josiah Stanford, it became a famous center of winemaking.

[10]George Woods was born in New Bedford on August 28, 1838. His medical career started in 1861, and he served in the Navy during the Civil War. In 1866 he was transferred to the West Coast, where he spent the remaining years of his life. He was stationed at Mare Island on San Francisco Bay in 1871-73, 1878-82, and

George Woods, a Navy physician since the Civil War, at the latter's home on Mare Island.[10] There he died on February 6, 1880, in his fifty-fifth year.

I.C. Woods was survived by his wife and three children. His funeral was held at Mare Island. The service was conducted by Rev. W. Simonton Cochrane, pastor of the Espiscopal Church of the Ascension in Vallejo. Among those attending the service were Woods' widow, his sons, Charles and Robert, and his uncle, Frank Woods; also Mr. and Mrs. R.E. Doyle, John T. Doyle, Mr. and Mrs. Eugene Casserly, and a number of others who had come from San Francisco.[11] Woods' daughter, Anne, wife of Dr. David Oldham Lewis, who like George Woods was a Navy physician, was unable to be present, as she was traveling to her husband's new assignment in Alaska.[12]

Mrs. I.C. Woods continued to live in San Francisco. In the second social register of the city, the *Social Manual of 1884*, she is listed with R.E. Doyle at his Pine Street residence on Nob Hill. Also living with

---

1886- 90. In 1892 he was again at Mare Island as officer in charge of the Navy hospital. Dr. Woods was steadily promoted and was noted for his numerous reports compiled during his voyages on the Pacific Ocean. These included a treatise on leprosy written when he was stationed on the Hawaiian island of Molokai (*The Records of Living Officers of the U.S. Navy and Marine Corps* [Philadelphia, 1894], p. 274). He died in 1902.

A window at St. Peters Chapel, Mare Island, donated by his widow, Florence B., remains as a memorial to him (Ernest D. Wichels, *History of St. Peters Chapel* [Mare Island, 1980], p. 82). St. Peters, completed in 1901, is the second oldest chapel in the Navy still serving the military.

[11]*Vallejo Evening Chronicle*, Feb. 19, 1880. The "Rev. Cochran" in the newspaper article is W. Simonton Cochrane, according to Rev. D.O. Kelley in his *History of the Diocese of California* (San Francisco, 1915) pp. 379, 411. Cochrane arrived in California in 1878 and died in 1883.

[12]*The Records of Living Officers of the U.S. Navy and Marine Corps* (Philadelphia, 1894), p. 289. Dr. Lewis entered the Navy from Pennsylvania in 1874. Later in the 1880s the Lewis family lived in San Francisco.

Mrs. Isaiah C. Woods, according to the California Historical
Society photographic department.
Courtesy: California Historical Society.

them were Miss Kate and Miss Florence Woods, possibly her granddaughters. Mrs. R.E. Doyle, I.C. Woods' sister Sarah, died July 7, 1883; her funeral was held at St. Mary's Cathedral (now Old St. Mary's on California Street) only a month after Eugene Casserly was buried (June 14) from the same cathedral. Mrs. I.C. Woods' name last appeared in the *San Francisco Directory of 1886*. R.E. Doyle died in 1898, his brother, John T., in 1906.

Mrs. I.C. Woods died in San Francisco on February 11, 1905. Her son Charles C. had predeceased her.[13] Her daughter, Anne Lewis, lived in New York; Anne's husband died in Honolulu in 1905, the same year as Mrs. Woods, and was buried at Mare Island.[14]

Woods' son Robert J. lived in San Francisco. He joined the Bohemian Club in 1884 and served as a director in the early 1890s. He was also a member of the California Tennis Club, while his wife belonged to the exclusive San Francisco Town and Country Club.

A grandson, Edward Churchill Woods, served in the United States Navy. A granddaughter, Mrs. J. Bebb, lived in New York.[15]

It is difficult to judge I.C. Woods. If he had remained in New Bedford, unambitious, he would probably have had a calm and prosperous career in charge of a crockery and glassware store. His enterprising nature, however, led him to a life filled with a series of ventures, none of which brought him the riches he sought.

The newspapers of the 1850s and early 1860s were

---

[13]*San Francisco Chronicle*, Feb. 11, 1905.

[14]Lewis was born in England in 1851 and died in Honolulu in 1905, according to his tombstone at Mare Island.

[15]Philip Alexandre and Charles P. Hamm, *History of San Mateo County* (Burlingame, CA, 1916), p. 50.

most acrimonious in their treatment of Woods. His performance during the closing of Adams & Co. was not the best. It may be that William T. Sherman was correct when he wrote: "I.C. Woods flummoxed and floundered beyond his depth and comprehension."[16]

Woods' role with the San Antonio and San Diego Mail Line has been praised, while his part in the El Paso and Fort Yuma Wagon Road brought him dishonor. His actions were free from charges of dubious dealings in St. Louis during the controversial "One Hundred Days" with Fremont. His last years, while not successful financially, again showed his intense efforts to succeed.

Two noted historians have written regarding the motives of many pioneers. Dr. J.S. Holliday quoted a miner: "Money is our only stimulus and the getting of it our only pleasure. Never was any country so well calculated to cultivate the spirit of avarice."[17]

Another interpreter of this period, Kevin Starr, wrote: "The energy of the Gold Rush, the thirst for excitement and the habit of speculation remained part of the California temperament... money making became a fixed mania."[18] These opinions may in part explain I.C. Woods.

Finally, the impression of Woods, written in 1873 by contemporaries who knew him, T.A. Barry and B.A. Patton, seems just to one who has spent several years tracing his life and considering his character and activities.

---

[16]Letter to A.S. Turner, February 28, 1855, quoted in Dwight Clarke, *William Tecumseh Sherman, Gold Rush Banker* (San Francisco, 1969), p. 116. "Flummox" is slang for "bewilder, confuse."

[17]J.S. Holliday, *The World Rushed In* (New York, 1981), p. 401.

[18]Kevin Starr, *America and the California Dream* (New York, 1973), p. 67.

Isaiah C. Woods, who was the manager of Adams & Co.'s
banking house in San Francisco, was never understood or
appreciated by the general public. He is one of the ablest
business men ever in San Francisco. Had he been allowed to
settle the affairs of Adams & Co., it would have been far
better for the creditors of that firm. Mr. Woods is a man who
would, in any other city than San Francisco, have been
considered a valuable acquisition to its business men — its
men of brains — its great movers and workers — and not only
permitted, but requested to remain where he was — would
have been aided and cooperated with, in continuing the
house of Adams & Co.

   Mr. Woods can originate any enterprise, clearly and
feasibly, which, if carried out in detail, under his direction,
will eventuate prosperously for the public and the projectors
of the scheme. There was too much misrepresentation,
prejudice and excitement at the time of the Adams & Co.
failure; it was a very bad affair, but ought not to have been
charged to I.C. Woods in all its disastrous mismanagement.
Such men, with a fair chance, make business and prosperity
for any city; and any such men's withdrawal, voluntary or
compulsory, from business, is a public misfortune.[19]

I.C. Woods' life in San Francisco was similar to
many other adventurers who hastened to the gold-rush
city, meeting with great success at first, only to have
their dreams collapse. Woods' career after the Adams &
Co. debacle was tragic, as again and again he appeared
to be embarked on a notable enterprise only to have the
project fail. Nevertheless, he will always be remembered as one of the most interesting argonauts who
rushed to San Francisco during its golden years.

---

   [19]T.A. Barry and B.A. Patton, *Men and Memories of San Francisco in the Spring of
'50* (San Francisco, 1873), pp. 249-50.

Appendix

The bank failures and economic chaos in San Francisco and the mining country in 1855 (described in Chapter 2) had an impact upon the population far beyond simple economics. Heroes and villains were created in the public mind, and these in turn proved to be an inspiration to the troubadours who toured the countryside.

The first, "California Bank Robbers," was printed in 1858 in *Put's Golden Songster* (see Chapter 2, footnote 49). The second, "Pop Goes the Weasel - New Version," was published in *The Gold Digger's Song Book* in 1856, by Mart Taylor.

CALIFORNIA BANK ROBBERS

The California People are determined if they find,
    Another such a band of robbers
As the banking firm of Adams, from beginning to the end,
    They will hang them as they have a lot of rowdies.

Chorus (following each verse)
So be careful all you rowdies and you rich banker thieves,
Or the California people will hang you, I believe.

They agreed among themselves they could easy make a pile,
    By stealing all they had on deposit;
They would do it by a failure, and be honest all the while —
    Then a million and a half — what of it?

The Merchant rushed in looking whiter than a sheet,
    The Miner came tearing like a bull dog;
Poor old washerwomen crying in the street,
    And Johnny Bull croaking like a bull frog.

Women carried round on the shoulders of the crowd
    Really was a sight very funny;
Legs all bare, though they didn't seem to care,
    They were bound to have a sight for their money.

The blind man said to the bankers, "I'm poor —
    Surely, man, you don't intend to rob me!"
The Chinaman said as they kicked him out the door,
    "Me no shabee, John, me no shabee!"

In came the shad-bellied Yankee out of breath,
    And he says, "Old feller, goll-dam-ye!"
Then along came Pike, saying, "I'll be the death
    Of you bank robbers, dog-on-ye!"

I.C. Wood *sabed* something very strange,
    So he *vamosed*, though he knew it wouldn't sound well.
He hid among the hills in the Contra Costa range,
    With a bag of bogus dust — what a scoundrel!

Ladies in the jam now and then were heard to say,
    "Oh Lordy-massy, how you squeeze us!"
When a Jew got to the counter, he began without delay,
    "Vel, I vants my money, by Sheesus!"

Frenchmen they were squawking like a flock of hungry geese;
    Vainly did they parley-voo-de-ding-dong.
Sauer-Kraut was looking for a Justice of the Peace,
    To send all the Yankee thieves to Hong Kong.

Adams he declared that his name was just a sale,
    To give "The House" a wholesome reputation;
I.C. Wood says they both agreed to fail,
    And swindle all o' God's creation.

The bank robber Wood had to hunt another hole,
    For many were determined they would kill him;
So he gathered up the money he maliciously had stole,
    And away went the black hearted villain.

Their "Receiver" is a thief — you can see it by his looks —
    And the Lord knows what he wouldn't swear to;
After robbing all the money, why he then stole the books,
    And a thousand other things that would scare you.

They were thrown into the bay 'bout the middle of the night,
  By the long-eared, fish-faced Cohen;
And the moment they were found he was quickly out of sight,
  For he thought it was time to be goin'.

Pop Goes the Weasel — New Version

Since I have got to sing again.
  I'll try my best to please you,
And let you have a little strain,
  Of pop goes the weasel.

Chorus (after each verse)
All around the chicken coop,
The rooster chased the weasel,
The gobbler strutted round the yard
But pop went the weasel.

Harry Meiggs has run away,
  I'll tell you what's the reason,
He forged a lot of city scrip,
  And pop went the weasel.

The Adams firm was good enough,
  And flourished for a season.
They got the people's money, and
  Pop went the weasel.

You get upon a river boat.
  The flues begin to scissle,
They get too large a head of steam,
  And pop goes the weasel.

And down in Nicaragua,
  Bill Walker's raised the *divil*,
If Uncle Sam gets hold of him,
  Pop goes the weasel.

You go and get a pretty wife,
  And settle for a season.
Some dandy fellow comes along,
  And pop goes the weasel.

Index

Compiled by Anna Marie and Everett Gordon Hager